Study hard what interests you the most in the most undisciplined, irreverent, and original manner possible.

– Richard Feynman

The more basic knowledge you have, the less new knowledge you have to get.

– Charlie Munger

MASTERING LIFE'S FOUNDATIONS: A Guide to Essential Skills

B Madhusudan Rao

ISBN

Paperback 979-8-89632-408-9
Hardcase 979-8-89699-353-7

Contents

Introduction 9

Chapter 1: Planning 17

Chapter 2: Time Management 51

Chapter 3: Communication 81

Chapter 4: Behavior 103

Chapter 5: Focus 125

Chapter 6: Growth Mindset 145

Chapter 7: Going Beyond 165

Chapter 8: Learnings 179

Summary of concepts / models / frameworks that will be useful   187

Chapter 9: Credibility 191

Conclusion 207

References 213

To think clearly, understand the basics.

If you're memorizing advanced concepts without being able to re-derive them as needed, you're lost.

— **Naval Ravikanth**

German folk saying: "We are too soon old and too late smart."

In the journey of self-improvement, mastering fundamental skills is key to personal and professional success. This book serves as a comprehensive guide to developing essential skills that will empower you to navigate life's challenges with confidence and resilience.

Introduction

This book is not about teaching or giving sermons or trying to teach you something new. All of the skills that I mentioned here are known to mankind long, long ago. I've made references to Benjamin Franklin, John Locke, and several others who have practiced planning, time management, and have studied human behavior in addition to myriad things they did in their lives and the many things that are known to all of us, but the problem (or the opportunity) is, we know everything and seldom try to practice.

I made an attempt to outline several skills that are very important. In each of the skills, I tried to capture the concepts* and tried to include some anecdotes to motivate you. This way, once you master the basic skills that are required, you will be able to attempt and further improve on other concepts and techniques and be even more successful.

The concepts or the summary of the same concept may appear several times when we discuss each skill. This is only to prove that same concepts can be applied when practicing each skill.

Before we proceed further, let's understand what success is. Success is something that you have to define yourself. Success, for some, is becoming an entrepreneur, a CEO, coming out with a product or service, providing jobs to a number of people, becoming a sportsperson, a musician, studying well, reaching a top position in a chosen career, making money, being perfectly healthy, earning enough to be peaceful, or being a credible human being, and the list goes on.

Whatever may be the definition of success, the skills that are required are fundamental in nature, and this book is all about how to be aware of the skills. Once the awareness evolves, how do we use these skills to achieve whatever we have in mind.

*The concepts that I have captured in each chapter may be boring to read, or sometimes you may not be able to practice all of them. However, it is important to be *aware* and keep these at the back of your mind and use them as necessary. In fact, I have captured all of these in such a manner that you can skip them for a while and proceed with the flow and can always come back and revisit them to gain a better understanding.

The skills that have been captured here are so basic that I doubt without mastering any of these basic skills, it's very difficult to achieve success in any field. I tried to capture the skills in a systematic manner, that's all. There is nothing new.

These skills are so basic that they apply to everyone, including a student, homemaker, someone who wants to move up the corporate ladder, or someone who wants to make it big in the field that one likes, whether it's arts, sciences, management, or whatever.

The way I outlined all the skills is that they are so interconnected. It starts with planning and ends with learning, and as you complete each chapter, you will be able to understand the connection, and finally it all leads to achieving credibility in whatever one does.

Credibility is something that is so important for each individual. It builds the kind of trust and confidence that will prepare you for the world, and this is very, very important. Hence, it is a common theme among all the skills that I described to achieve credibility for yourself first, and then for the family and society, if you care.

Each chapter starts by defining what that skill is all about and then focuses on one or two fundamental concepts only so that the reader is not inundated with the number of concepts available under each skill. I tried to identify the most important ones, and my endeavor is to actually make things very clear about how to imbibe those concepts and apply. I also made references to other concepts so that once you master these basic concepts and apply them, you can move on to reading other concepts and apply them eventually in your life.

I emphasize, nothing that I described in this book is new. I've made numerous references to things that were already said either in the form of books, podcasts, blogs, or some facts and quotes from history so that one is able to connect and also, most importantly, realize that all this information about the skills already exists.

All of us know that the skills* are necessary to make it big in life. It's a paradox that all these skills are so simple that it's very difficult to implement in a consistent manner in our daily life.

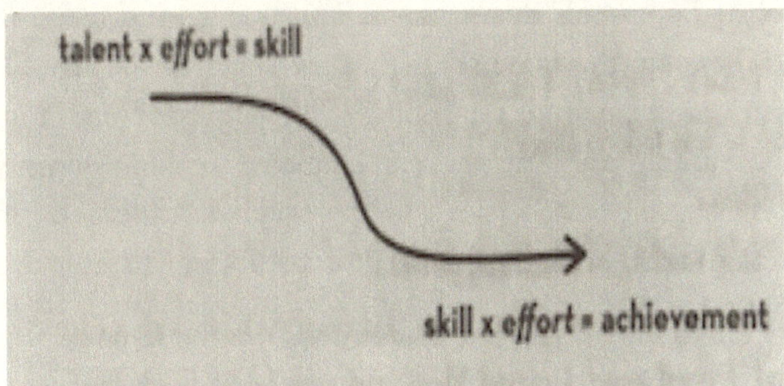

from

Grit: The Power of Passion and Perseverance

- Angela Duckworth

The book tries to offer some simple solutions so that these skills ultimately become a habit in our daily lives.

Let's dwell a little more on why these skills are difficult to practice even though they look very simple. As it often happens with the diet, even the simplest diet is very difficult to follow and to follow consistently for whatever time period that we choose to practice that diet. The same thing happens with the skills. They look very simple. Sometimes you wonder what is so great about practicing the skills and mastering the skills, but being very consistent with whatever I outlined about all these skills is the key. To make them a habit. That's not to dishearten the reader. Once you imbibe the basic concepts and try to apply them in the format and in the methodology that I described in each chapter, it becomes easy. All I can say is that read each chapter with an open mind as if you are a beginner, even though you may be very experienced in life. You must have already gone through several books or podcasts or blogs about the same topics.

Try to read with an open mind and try to see how each of the skills is connected. In the end, you will be able to appreciate the connection between all the skills and you will be motivated to practice these skills. These are the basic skills that a parent can practice and try to imbibe in children. These are the same skills that a teacher in the school, college, or university can help students imbibe so that they become ready for life ahead. These are also very useful for an employee working anywhere, either in factories or in corporate settings, to appreciate the skills and consistently follow them to make their life easy and successful in whatever they do.

In my childhood, I heard a Telugu song by the famous poet Sri Sri, and it goes something like this. Don't just wait and hope that someone will come and solve all your problems, and don't just go to sleep and forget the truth. The truth is that no one will ever come and save you. No one will ever come and teach you. It's you; you have to make all the effort to realize your dreams and become what you want in life.

As it happens in life, we all come with some background, some with inherited properties, some with dreams in their eyes, but one thing that this book will solve is that it makes you realize your own potential once you imbibe all the concepts, which are very fundamental to succeed in life.

What if I tell you that you would drop words like busy? I don't have time. I don't know what to do. It's so boring. You will drop all that from your vocabulary, once you finish reading this book.

Also, these basic concepts or skills mentioned in this book sort of act as a preventive measure for securing your future. Without the understanding of these basic skills and concepts, I doubt you'll be able to navigate your life or career smoothly, but once you are even a bit aware, followed by fundamental understanding and later mastering the skills, your life would be very easy going toward the direction you chose to go.

As they say, attention is a limited resource. Rapidly switching your attention between tasks is inefficient because it takes a lot of cognitive energy, as our brain can only focus on one thing at a time. Charlie Munger once said, "I did not succeed in life by intelligence, I succeeded because of a long attention span. The idea of multitasking my way to glory has never occurred to me."

Try to understand what works and what doesn't and you can only know what works and what doesn't work, unless you learn from what you're doing, so do learn and understand what works and repeat

Again, if something works, then keep repeating it as you know that it's working well, so the fundamental algorithm in life is to repeat what works

> "If you're serious about changing your life, you'll find a way.
> If not, you'll find an excuse."
>
> **– Jen Sincero**

If you want to fail, tell everybody your plans.

If you want to succeed, keep your mouth shut.

Decide, don't discuss.

•••

Chapter 1
Planning

"Most big, deeply satisfying accomplishments in life take at least 5 years to achieve. This can include building a business, cultivating a loving relationship, writing a book, getting in the best shape of your life, raising a family, and more.

Five years is a long time. It is much slower than most of us would like. If you accept the reality of slow progress, you have every reason to take action today. If you resist the reality of slow progress, 5 years from now you'll simply be 5 years older and still looking for a shortcut.

– James Clear

Introduction

"By failing to prepare, you are preparing to fail."

– Benjamin Franklin

Planning is fundamental to achieving success in both personal and professional life. I like to think of planning as the father of all skills. Those who practice planning tend to be more successful and meet their targets more often than those who don't. I also see planning as the roadmap that guides me toward my desired destination. Without it, I may find myself lost in a labyrinth of possibilities, unsure which path to take. This chapter is about understanding the importance of planning and how it can help you reach your goals. When discussing planning, it's essential to consider long-term, medium-term, and short-term planning. Long-term planning gives you a broad vision of your future, which you can then break down into medium-term goals and short-term tasks. This way, you have a clear path to follow, even if you need to adjust your steps.

> "Think in terms of decades, and act in terms of days."
>
> **– Kevin Kelly**

Planning involves visualizing your future and developing a plan to achieve it. While many tools, techniques, and templates are available, this book focuses on giving you a simple format and practical methods to build planning skills. We'll look at planning for different aspects of life, like personal and professional, and our aspirations. While most daily aspects force or encourage us to plan for our personal or professional lives, many people, including so-called successful individuals, often fail to plan for their aspirations. A person may be successful professionally or have a wonderful personal life. Yet, they may regret not planning for their aspirations—whether it's becoming a singer, learning a new art, or traveling to desired places. The main takeaway from this planning exercise is that one should be obsessive about planning for their aspirations and include it in all planning they do for their life. Most of us are more disappointed by the things we didn't achieve or do than the things we did. The more ambitious the aspiration, the more opportunities come your way, and sticking to a standard planning process will yield better results.

In this chapter, we'll get back to the basics of planning. After reviewing many books, articles, lectures, websites, apps, and templates, I've found a simple template that works best: a calendar format. We'll start with a small exercise to illustrate how planning is done and why it's crucial. Let's begin with a monthly planning exercise. Take a white paper (it might seem old-fashioned, but trust me, it works) and write down all areas of your planning: self, family, health, wealth, hobbies, entertainment, and miscellaneous. You might notice some overlapping in these areas, but let us proceed for now, and you will appreciate the exercise at the end. List what you want to accomplish in each area for the month. Once you list everything you want to achieve in each area, prioritize each area by assigning priorities from 1 to 5.

After assigning priorities for each area, fill the dates in the calendar for the month accordingly. Now you have monthly planning done, and one of the most important things you must do is make copies of the same and display them prominently either in your wardrobe (always preferred), in your room, or at your place of work. It might look simple, but it has a powerful effect. Having planned for the month, let us look at how to translate the same into day-to-day practice, achieving and monitoring in the next chapter related to time management (how to use a calendar daily). Planning is important, but not everything will go as planned. Be prepared to make changes and adapt. Use a different color pen to update your plan as needed. Highlight key focuses to ensure you don't forget them. Monitoring progress is essential, and we'll learn more about this in the next chapter on time management. Long-term planning follows the same procedure. Write down what you want to achieve at the end of each year and break it down into monthly and weekly activities. Remember, what you do daily will help you realize your aspirations. Planning ensures you don't just dream but take actionable steps toward your goals.

> "Empty your brain before bed with journaling and planning."
>
> **– Dan Koe.**

Planning is a simple yet powerful tool. It prevents you from wasting time and helps you focus on what's important. As we move forward, we'll explore various aspects of planning and how they contribute to your success.

Core Concepts

It's important to understand the core concepts that underpin effective planning. These concepts provide the foundation for creating a structured and successful plan. By mastering these principles, you can ensure that your planning process is comprehensive, adaptable, and geared toward achieving your goals.

Goal Setting

Setting clear and well-defined goals is the first step toward achieving success. When we know exactly what we want to achieve, it gives us direction and purpose. It's like having a map with specific coordinates to follow, making our journey straightforward and focused.

Why Goal Setting is Important

When I think about goal setting, I imagine a journey without a clear destination. It's easy to get lost or go in circles. But when we set specific goals, we create a path that leads us directly to our desired outcome. Goals act as a guide, helping us stay on track and measure our progress. In planning, it's crucial to ensure that what we plan now and what we plan to do in the future align with where we want to go and what we want to achieve. It's essentially filtering out everything else and figuring out where to go through the plan.

How to Set Clear Goals

- Be Specific: Instead of saying, "I want to get fit," set a specific goal like, "I want to run a 5K in three months." Being specific helps you know exactly what you are working toward.

- Make it Measurable: Ensure your goal has a clear marker of success. For example, "I want to save ₹ 50,000 in six months." This way, you can track your progress and see how close you are to achieving it.

- Set Achievable Goals: Your goals should be realistic and attainable. It's great to aim high, but setting impossible goals can lead to frustration. Break down larger goals into smaller, manageable steps.

- Be Relevant: Your goals should align with your broader life plans and values. If your main priority is career growth, setting a goal to learn a new work-related skill is relevant.

- Time-bound: Give yourself a deadline. Having a timeframe creates a sense of urgency and helps you stay motivated. For example, "I will complete my certification course in 6 months."

The Benefits of Clear Goals

Clear goals help us focus our efforts and resources on what truly matters. They provide motivation and a sense of purpose. When we achieve our goals, no matter how small, we gain confidence and the momentum to pursue even bigger ones. Goal setting isn't just about achieving big dreams. It's also about managing our everyday lives better. Whether personal, professional, or aspirational, setting clear goals is a powerful tool that guides us toward success.

Examples of Goal Setting

Let's take some examples from daily life to illustrate how setting specific goals can make a significant difference.

- Personal Goals: Suppose you want to improve your health. Instead of a vague goal like "I want to be healthier," try something specific like "I will walk 10,000 steps daily for the next 3 months." This gives you a clear target and a way to measure your progress.

- Professional Goals: If you want a promotion at work, set a goal such as "I will complete a professional certification in my field within the next year." This goal is specific, measurable, achievable, relevant, and time-bound.

- Financial Goals: Planning to save money for a big purchase? Set a goal like, "I will save ₹ 5,000 every month for the next year to buy a new laptop." Breaking down the amount into smaller monthly targets makes the goal more manageable.

- Aspirational Goals: Perhaps you've always wanted to learn a new language. Instead of saying, "I want to learn Tamil," set a goal like, "I will complete an online Tamil course in 6 months and practice speaking with a language partner weekly."

Conclusion

To start with goal setting, take some time to think about what you actually want to achieve. Write down your goals and ensure they meet the specific, measurable, achievable, relevant, and time-bound criteria. Break them down into smaller steps and keep track of your progress. By setting clear and well-defined goals, you can navigate your way toward success in both your personal and professional life. Whether it's improving your health, advancing your career, or achieving financial stability, having a clear plan makes all the difference. Remember, the journey toward achieving your goals is as important as reaching the destination.

Strategy Development

Developing a solid strategy is crucial for achieving your long-term goals. Strategies act as the blueprint that guides your actions and decisions, ensuring that every step you take aligns with your overall objectives. Here's how to create effective strategies that are flexible and aligned with your long-term vision.

Flexible and Adaptable Strategies

One of the critical aspects of a successful strategy is its ability to adapt to changing circumstances. Life is unpredictable, and rigid plans can often fall apart when faced with unexpected challenges. Therefore, it's essential to develop flexible strategies that can be adjusted as needed. Strategy development reminds me of the saying, "Think in terms of decades, and act in terms of days." This means having a long-term vision while being adaptable in your daily actions. For example, if your long-term goal is to become an accomplished musician, your strategy might include daily practice sessions, attending workshops, and performing at local events. If an unexpected opportunity arises, like a chance to collaborate with a well-known artist, your strategy should be flexible enough to accommodate this new opportunity.

Flexibility in strategy allows you to respond effectively to unforeseen events and seize new opportunities. It's like driving a car on a long journey. You know your final destination, but you may need to take detours, change routes, or stop for fuel along the way. The key is to remain adaptable and not get discouraged by changes in the plan.

Invert Principle

An important method in strategy development is the use of the invert principle. When planning, consider what not to do instead of only focusing on what to do. Think about potential pitfalls and plan to avoid them. Similar to a Failure Premortem, this approach involves anticipating what could go wrong and working backward to prevent those failures. This method helps create a more robust plan with a higher probability of success.

Aligning Resources with Long-Term Objectives

Strategic planning is not just about setting goals; it's also about aligning your resources to achieve those goals. Resources include your time, money, and skills. Efficient resource allocation ensures that you use what you have in the best possible way to move closer to your objectives. For instance, if your goal is to start your own business, you must plan how to allocate your savings, time, and efforts effectively. This might mean setting aside a portion of your monthly income to build a startup fund, dedicating specific hours of the day to work on your business plan, and acquiring new skills to help you manage your business better.

A clear strategy helps you identify the resources you need and how to use them efficiently. It's like being a chef preparing a meal. You need to know what ingredients you have, what additional ingredients you need, and how to combine them to create the final dish. Proper resource allocation ensures you have everything you need to achieve your goals.

> **"A paradox of life is that the greatest returns come in the long term, but the opportunity cost of moving slowly is huge.**
>
> **Long-term thinking is not slow-acting.**
>
> **Act quickly on things that compound. Never let a day pass without doing something that will benefit you in a decade."**
>
> **– James Clear**

Benefits of a Clear Strategy

A clear strategy provides several benefits:

- Focus: It helps you concentrate on what's important and avoid distractions.

- Efficiency: By knowing precisely what needs to be done, you can use your time and resources more effectively.

- Motivation: A clear path to follow keeps you motivated and engaged.

- Measurable Progress: A well-defined strategy allows you to track your progress and make necessary adjustments.

For example, consider the construction of the Great Wall of China. This monumental task required a clear and strategic plan that spanned centuries. Each dynasty contributed to the construction, and the strategy evolved to address various challenges, such as geographical obstacles and resource allocation. This long-term strategic planning ensured that the efforts of multiple generations were aligned toward a common goal.

Creating Your Strategy

To create an effective strategy, start by identifying your long-term goals. Break these down into smaller, manageable milestones. For each milestone, determine the needed resources and plan how to acquire or allocate them. Be prepared to adjust your strategy as you progress and as circumstances change.

Here's a simple approach to developing a flexible strategy:

1. Set Clear Goals: Define what you want to achieve long term.

2. Identify Resources: Determine what resources you have and what you will need.

3. Create Milestones: Break down your long-term goal into smaller, achievable milestones.

4. Plan for Flexibility: Integrate flexibility into your plans to adjust to new opportunities or challenges.

5. Review and Adjust: Regularly review your progress and adjust your strategy as needed.

A good strategy also considers potential risks and how to mitigate them. For instance, if you plan to save ☒ 50,000 in six months, think about what could go wrong – an unexpected expense, for example. Have a contingency plan in place to address such setbacks without derailing your overall goal.

Conclusion

Developing a flexible and well-aligned strategy is essential for achieving your long-term goals. By planning strategically, you ensure that your efforts are focused and efficient, and you remain adaptable to changes and opportunities that come your way. A good strategy guides you toward your objectives and empowers you to navigate the journey with confidence and resilience.

Resource Allocation

Efficient resource allocation is crucial in any planning process. It's about using your available resources – time, money, and skills – in the best possible way to achieve your goals. When you allocate resources effectively, you ensure you are not wasting valuable assets and are on the right path to reaching your objectives.

The Importance of Resource Allocation

Think of resource allocation as managing a budget. Just like you wouldn't spend all your money in one place, you shouldn't use all your time or skills on one task. By distributing resources wisely, you can balance various tasks and responsibilities without feeling overwhelmed. For instance, let's say you aim to learn a new programming language while maintaining your current job and spending time with your family. Efficient resource allocation means planning your schedule to dedicate specific hours to learning, working, and family time without neglecting these important areas.

Distributing Time, Money and Skills

1) Time:

- Time Blocking: Allocate specific blocks of time for different activities. For example, you could dedicate mornings to work, afternoons to learning, and evenings to family.

- Setting Priorities: Use tools like to-do lists and calendars to prioritize your tasks and manage your time effectively. This helps ensure that you focus on what truly matters and do not get sidetracked.

- Writing Down Areas: Identify areas of your life that require attention. These can include self, family, health, wealth, hobbies, entertainment, and miscellaneous. Having written down these areas, list what you want to accomplish each month.

2) Money:

- Budgeting: Create a budget that aligns with your goals. If your goal is to learn a new skill, allocate funds for courses, books, or software that you might need.

- Saving and Investing: Ensure you save a part of your income for future needs or unexpected expenses. Investing in resources that will aid your goals can also be a part of your financial planning.

3) Skills:

- Leveraging Strengths: Identify your strengths and use them to your advantage. If you are good at time management, use this skill to organize your tasks efficiently.

- Skill Development: Allocate time and resources to develop new skills that are necessary for achieving your goals. This might include taking courses, attending workshops, or self-study.

Example of Resource Allocation

Let's take an example of someone planning to start a small business. Efficient resource allocation would involve:

- Time: Setting aside specific hours each day to work on business plans, research, and networking.

- Money: Creating a budget for initial investments, marketing, and contingency funds.

- Skills: Using existing skills like marketing and financial management and learning new skills such as digital marketing or product design.

To make it more practical, write down areas such as self, family, health, wealth, hobbies, entertainment, and miscellaneous. Under each category, list what you want to accomplish during the month. For example:

- Self: Read 2 books.

- Family: Spend quality time every weekend.

- Health: Exercise for 30 minutes daily.

- Wealth: Save ₹ 5,000 this month.

- Hobbies: Practice the guitar for an hour every day.

- Entertainment: Watch one movie per week.

- Miscellaneous: Declutter the house.

The Benefits of Effective Resource Allocation

When resources are allocated properly, it leads to:

- Increased Productivity: You can accomplish more in less time by focusing on high-priority tasks.

- Reduced Stress: Knowing that you have a plan for your time, money, and skills reduces anxiety and helps you stay focused.

- Better Decision Making: With a clear view of your resources, you can make informed decisions that align with your goals.

Conclusion

Efficient resource allocation is a cornerstone of effective planning. By identifying priorities, writing down your goals, and allocating resources thoughtfully, you ensure that each aspect of your plan is well-supported. This approach helps you stay organized, focused, and ready to tackle your goals with confidence. Remember, resource allocation is an ongoing process that requires regular review and adjustment to keep you on the path to success.

Risk Assessment

When we embark on any plan, identifying potential risks is crucial. This step ensures that we are prepared for any obstacles that may come our way. By assessing risks, we can develop strategies to mitigate them, ensuring a smoother path toward our goals.

Identifying Potential Risks

First, it's essential to identify potential risks that could impact our plans. This process involves brainstorming and listing out all possible obstacles that might arise. For instance, if you're planning a project at work, think about what could go wrong: delays in supply delivery, technical issues, or even team members falling ill. Similarly, in personal plans, consider factors like unexpected expenses, time constraints, or personal commitments that might interfere. One effective method to identify risks is to conduct a SWOT analysis (Strengths, Weaknesses, Opportunities, Threats). This helps in understanding both internal and external factors that could influence the success of your plan. By recognizing these threats early, we can devise strategies to counter them.

Consider an example from daily life: planning a family vacation. Risks could include bad weather, travel delays, or sudden illness. By identifying these risks, you can plan for alternate activities, ensure travel insurance is in place, or keep essential medicines handy. Writing down areas such as self, family, health, wealth, hobbies, entertainment, and miscellaneous activities, as well as listing potential risks for each, can also be very helpful. This comprehensive approach ensures that you cover all bases and are prepared for various scenarios.

Benefits of Proactive Risk Management

Once we've identified potential risks, the next step is to develop a proactive approach to manage them. Proactive risk management involves anticipating possible problems and preparing solutions in advance. This approach has several benefits:

1. Minimizes Surprises: When we plan for potential risks, we are less likely to be caught off guard. This reduces the chances of being derailed by unexpected challenges.

2. Saves Time and Resources: By preparing for risks in advance, we can save time and resources that might otherwise be spent on emergency measures. This allows us to stay focused on our goals.

3. Increases Confidence: Knowing that we have contingency plans in place boosts our confidence. We can proceed with our plans knowing that we are prepared for any eventuality.

> "Plans are nothing; planning is everything."
>
> **– Dwight D. Eisenhower**

Planning for the Unexpected

As the saying goes, "Planning is important, but the most important part of every plan is to plan on the plan not going according to plan." This highlights the need for flexibility and adaptability in our planning process. It's rare for everything to go exactly as planned, so it's vital to have backup plans ready. For example, if you're planning an event, consider what you would do if the weather turned bad, if a key speaker cancels, or if there are technical issues. Having contingency plans for these scenarios ensures that you can still achieve your goals despite the setbacks.

Additionally, highlight and capture the things you really want to focus on in your calendar so that you don't forget them. This helps in monitoring progress and making necessary adjustments. Planning for unexpected situations also involves regularly reviewing and updating your plans. This dynamic approach ensures that your plans remain relevant and effective, even as circumstances change.

Conclusion

Risk assessment is an integral part of any planning process. By identifying potential risks, preparing proactive strategies, and planning for the unexpected, we can navigate challenges more effectively. This not only helps us achieve our goals but also builds resilience and adaptability, which are key qualities for success in both our personal and professional lives.

> "Good fortune is what happens when opportunity meets planning."
>
> **– Thomas Edison**

Contingency Planning

Purpose of Contingency Planning

No matter how thorough our planning might be, there will always be unexpected challenges that arise. Contingency planning is about preparing for those "what if" scenarios. It's like having a backup plan ready for when things don't go as expected. This proactive approach ensures that we can still achieve our goals even when faced with unforeseen obstacles. Imagine you're on a road trip, and the main highway suddenly closes due to an accident. Without an alternative route in mind, you might waste hours trying to figure out a new path. Contingency planning is akin to having a map with multiple routes to your destination, ensuring you keep moving forward even when the unexpected happens.

Creating Backup Plans

When creating a contingency plan, start by identifying the critical components of your main plan that might face disruptions. Think about what could go wrong and how it would impact your goals. For example, if you're planning a major project at work, consider what would happen if a key team member fell ill or if there was a sudden budget cut. Once you've identified these potential issues, develop specific alternative strategies to address them. This might mean having additional team members trained to take over critical tasks or setting aside emergency funds to cover unexpected expenses. For instance, in your personal life, consider what you would do if your primary mode of transportation suddenly became unavailable. Having a backup plan, such as knowing the bus routes or having a friend you can call for a ride, can save you time and stress. Similarly, for a family vacation, having a contingency plan for bad weather might involve identifying indoor activities or alternative travel dates.

Resource Allocation for Contingency Plans

It's crucial to ensure that you have the necessary resources available to implement your contingency plans when needed. This means allocating a portion of your budget, time, and manpower specifically for these backup plans. By doing this, you can avoid scrambling for resources when things go awry. For instance, if you are managing a project, you might allocate some extra time in your schedule for potential delays or keep some budget aside for unforeseen expenses. This way, you are better prepared to handle any disruptions without significantly impacting your main plan. Consider a business setting where a company might keep a reserve fund for emergencies. This reserve can be used to address unexpected costs like equipment failure or urgent staffing needs. By planning for these potential disruptions, the business can maintain operations smoothly without significant interruptions.

Implementing Contingency Plans

Knowing when and how to activate your contingency plans is just as important as having them. Establish clear triggers that signal when it's time to switch to your backup plan. For example, if a project deadline is at risk due to delays, you should have a predetermined point at which you activate the contingency plan to bring in additional resources or adjust the timeline. Having a set procedure in place ensures that everyone involved knows what steps to take and when, reducing confusion and ensuring a smooth transition. For instance, in event planning, you might decide that if the weather forecast predicts rain within 48 hours of an outdoor event, you will move the event to an indoor venue. This clear trigger helps everyone involved to understand when and how to transition to the backup plan, ensuring the event goes smoothly regardless of weather conditions.

Examples of Contingency Planning

Let's look at some practical examples of contingency planning. In your personal life, think about having a backup plan for your daily commute. If your usual route is blocked, having an alternative route mapped out can save you time and stress. In a professional setting, imagine a company preparing for a product launch. They might have contingency plans for supply chain disruptions, such as alternative suppliers or backup inventory. These examples highlight how being prepared for the unexpected can keep you on track to meet your goals. Another example could be preparing for power outages. At home, you might have a generator or battery backups for essential devices. In a workplace, having backup servers or data storage solutions can ensure that critical operations continue uninterrupted even during power failures.

Benefits of Contingency Planning

One of the main benefits of contingency planning is stress reduction. Knowing that you have a plan in place for potential problems gives you peace of mind and helps you stay focused on your main goals. It also ensures continuity, meaning you can keep moving forward even when things go wrong. Additionally, having contingency plans increases your flexibility and resilience, making it easier to adapt to changes and recover from setbacks. For example, during a natural disaster, having a well-thought-out emergency plan can significantly reduce the chaos and ensure safety and quick recovery. This proactive approach not only mitigates risks but also enhances the confidence of everyone involved.

Reviewing and Updating Contingency Plans

Just like your main plans, contingency plans need regular reviews and updates. As circumstances change and new information becomes available, your backup plans might need adjustments. Make it a habit to revisit your contingency plans periodically to ensure they remain relevant and effective. This ongoing review process helps you stay prepared for any challenges that might come your way. For instance, if you have a financial contingency plan, you should review it annually to adjust for changes in your income, expenses, or financial goals. Similarly, a business might update its contingency plans based on new market trends or changes in the regulatory environment.

As Confucius noted, "If language is not correct, then what is said is not what is meant; if what is said is not what is meant, then what must be done remains undone." Precise language and clear communication are vital when developing contingency plans.

J.R.R. Tolkien warned, "It does not do to leave a live dragon out of your calculations, if you live near him." Identifying and managing risks through contingency planning is essential, as Thomas Edison said, "Success lies at the crossroad of preparation and opportunity."

As Benjamin Franklin advised, "By failing to prepare, you are preparing to fail." Contingency planning helps you bounce back from life's unexpected challenges with resilience and confidence.

Conclusion

In conclusion, contingency planning is an essential part of successful goal achievement. By preparing for the unexpected, you can handle disruptions with confidence and keep moving toward your objectives. Regular updates and reviews of your contingency plans ensure that you are always ready to tackle any challenges, making your overall plan more robust and resilient. By having these backup plans in place, you not only safeguard your goals but also enhance your ability to adapt and thrive in any situation.

Adapting Plans

The Importance of Flexibility

Even the best-laid plans can encounter unexpected challenges and changes. That's why flexibility in planning is essential. Just like a sailor adjusting sails to catch the wind and stay on course, we need to adapt our plans to changing circumstances. Flexibility allows us to respond to new information, unexpected obstacles, and shifting priorities without losing sight of our overall goals. When we make a plan, it's based on our current understanding and assumptions about the future. However, as time goes by, new developments can alter the landscape. Being adaptable means we're ready to pivot and modify our plans as needed, ensuring that we remain on track despite the changes around us.

Methods for Adapting Plans

Adapting plans involves being open to change and having a proactive approach to managing it. Here are some methods to help you adapt your plans effectively:

1. Regular Reviews: Schedule regular check-ins to review your progress and assess whether your plan is still aligned with your goals. This could be weekly, monthly, or quarterly, depending on the nature of your plan. Regular reviews help you identify any deviations early and make necessary adjustments promptly.

2. Feedback Loops: Establish feedback loops where you can gather input from relevant stakeholders, whether it's family members, colleagues, or mentors. Their perspectives can provide valuable insights and help you refine your plan.

3. Scenario Planning: Consider different scenarios that could impact your plan and develop strategies for each. This way, you're prepared for various outcomes and can switch to an alternative plan if needed. For example, if you're planning an event, have contingency plans for different weather conditions or unexpected cancellations.

4. Mindset of Flexibility: Cultivate a mindset that embraces change. When you approach planning with an open mind, you're more likely to see opportunities in challenges and adapt your strategies creatively.

The Role of Simplicity in Adaptation

One practical tip for adapting plans is to keep things simple. "The easiest way to do this is to erase the old plan and replace it with a new plan using a different color pen." This simple technique helps you visualize changes and keeps your planning process dynamic. It's a straightforward way to track adjustments and ensure that your new plan is clear and easy to follow. For instance, if you're managing a project and a key milestone is delayed, instead of getting overwhelmed, just take out your plan, cross out the old dates, and write in the new ones with a different color. This makes the changes stand out and helps everyone involved understand the new timeline.

Another simple method is to use sticky notes for planning. Each task or goal can be written on a separate note. When changes occur, you can easily move the notes around to reflect new priorities or deadlines. This method provides a visual and flexible way to adapt your plans on the fly.

Examples of Adaptation in Real Life

Consider the story of a startup company. Initially, they might have a detailed business plan outlining their market strategy, product development, and growth projections. However, as they launch and gather market feedback, they realize that customer preferences are different from what they anticipated. By being flexible and adapting their product features and marketing approach, they can better meet customer needs and achieve success. Another example is personal fitness goals. You might set a goal to run a marathon and create a training plan. However, if you sustain an injury, you need to adapt your plan to include rehabilitation and alternative exercises to stay active while you recover. By adjusting your plan, you can continue working toward your fitness goals without causing further harm.

The Benefits of Adapting Plans

Flexibility in planning offers numerous benefits. It helps you stay resilient in the face of challenges, reduces stress by providing clear alternatives, and enhances your ability to seize new opportunities that arise. When you're open to adapting your plans, you're better equipped to navigate the uncertainties of life and maintain progress toward your goals. Adapting plans also fosters a growth mindset, where you see setbacks and changes as opportunities to learn and improve. This mindset encourages continuous development and innovation, both personally and professionally.

> "Stay committed to your decisions, but stay flexible in your approach. It's the end you're after."
>
> **– Anthony Robbins**

Conclusion

In conclusion, adapting plans is crucial for effective planning and goal achievement. By being flexible, conducting regular reviews, incorporating feedback, and keeping your planning process simple, you can navigate changes smoothly and maintain your momentum. Remember, the ability to adapt is a strength that allows you to stay on course and achieve your goals, no matter what challenges come your way. Embrace flexibility as a key component of your planning strategy, and you'll be better prepared to handle the twists and turns of life's journey.

I would encourage you to write down your plans using the core concepts that you learned in this chapter.

These real-life plans will help you see how the core concepts we've discussed come to life in practical scenarios.

Key Tools and Techniques

Planning effectively involves using the right tools and techniques to organize your thoughts, goals, and actions. Here are some key tools and techniques that can help you plan better and achieve your goals more efficiently:

SMART Goals

Setting SMART goals is a foundational tool in effective planning. SMART stands for Specific, Measurable, Achievable, Relevant, and Time-bound. This method ensures that your goals are clear and reachable.

- Specific: Your goal should be clear and specific. For example, instead of saying, "I want to save money," you could say, "I want to save ₹ 50,000 in six months."

- Measurable: You need a way to measure your progress. This helps you stay on track and know when you've achieved your goal.

- Achievable: Your goal should be realistic and attainable. Setting impossible goals can lead to frustration.

- Relevant: Ensure your goal matters to you and aligns with other relevant goals. If it's not meaningful, you're less likely to stay motivated.

- Time-bound: Set a deadline to create a sense of urgency. For example, "I will save ₹ 50,000 by the end of December."

Using SMART goals helps you stay focused and provides a clear roadmap.

SWOT Analysis

A SWOT analysis helps you understand your Strengths, Weaknesses, Opportunities, and Threats. This tool is useful for both personal and professional planning.

- Strengths: Identify what you're good at. This could be skills, resources, or other advantages you have.

- Weaknesses: Recognize areas where you need improvement. Being honest about your weaknesses is crucial for growth.

- Opportunities: Look for external factors that you can capitalize on. This could be new trends, market demands, or personal opportunities.

- Threats: Be aware of potential challenges that could hinder your progress. This might include competition, changing circumstances, or other risks.

Conducting a SWOT analysis helps you create a balanced and realistic plan by leveraging your strengths and addressing your weaknesses.

PDCA Cycle (Plan-Do-Check-Act)

The PDCA cycle is a continuous improvement process that helps you plan and execute tasks systematically.

- Plan: Identify the goal and plan the steps needed to achieve it.

- Do: Implement the plan on a small scale to test its effectiveness.

- Check: Evaluate the results to see if the plan is working.

- Act: Based on the evaluation, make necessary adjustments and implement the plan on a larger scale if successful.

The PDCA cycle encourages ongoing improvement and helps you adapt to changes effectively.

Mind Mapping

Mind mapping is a visual tool for brainstorming and organizing ideas. It involves writing down a central concept and branching out related ideas in a non-linear format.

- Start with a central idea in the middle of the page.

- Draw branches to sub-ideas or related topics.

- Add more branches to explore each sub-idea further.

Mind mapping helps you see the connections between different ideas and can be a powerful tool for planning and creativity.

Inversion (Charlie Munger)

Charlie Munger, a renowned investor, practiced a concept called inversion. Instead of only thinking about what to do to achieve his goals, he would also think about what not to do. This approach helps identify potential pitfalls and avoid common mistakes. You can create a more robust plan by considering the negative aspects and how to prevent them.

Regret Minimization Framework (Jeff Bezos)

Jeff Bezos, the founder of Amazon, uses the Regret Minimization Framework to make decisions. This involves projecting yourself into the future and considering what you might regret not doing. Minimizing future regrets allows you to make decisions that align more closely with your long-term goals and values. This framework encourages taking calculated risks that you are less likely to regret later. Using these tools and techniques can greatly enhance your planning process. Whether you're setting goals, analyzing your situation, improving continuously, prioritizing tasks, or brainstorming ideas, these methods provide a structured approach to achieve your objectives. By incorporating these tools into your planning routine, you can create more effective, flexible, and realistic plans that guide you toward success.

> "Without leaps of imagination or dreaming, we lose the excitement of possibilities. Dreaming, after all, is a form of planning."
>
> – Gloria Steinem

Final Thoughts

Planning is a powerful tool that can significantly enhance your personal and professional life. By setting clear goals, developing flexible strategies, prioritizing tasks, allocating resources wisely, assessing risks, having contingency plans, and being adaptable, you can navigate life's challenges more effectively. Planning gives you the confidence to pursue your aspirations, knowing that you have a roadmap to guide you. It helps you stay focused, make better decisions, and achieve your objectives more efficiently. Remember, planning is not just about organizing your tasks but about visualizing your future and taking proactive steps to turn your dreams into reality.

Planning is often preparation. Preparing for the act, goal, or the eventual. Many people say life is unpredictable and even if you plan, something or other may come up and hence there is no point in planning. That's untrue. The luck or lack of preparation or planning may favor very few people and sometimes but not always. Frequent changes in planning or plans not going per our plan should tell us that we need to go back and have a re-look at our plans rather than completely abandoning them. In fact, it should force us to look at plans more carefully and plan again. We must be obsessive about our planning, and you will see a change in the way you think and experience things when careful planning starts working in your favor.

Planning fallacies are real, and we must be aware of those fallacies. Daniel Kahneman said, "We tend to overestimate our plans and forecasts." Michael J. Mauboussin noted, "We underestimate the time it will take to complete a task." Recognizing these fallacies can help you create more realistic plans and set achievable goals. As you incorporate these planning skills into your daily routine, you'll find yourself more prepared to handle whatever comes your way. Whether it's a personal goal, a professional milestone, or an aspirational dream, effective planning will empower you to achieve it. Keep your plans simple, flexible, and regularly updated to ensure they remain relevant and effective.

Embrace planning as a continuous, strategic approach to navigating life's challenges. By doing so, you set the stage for mastering the skills discussed in the next chapter. Remember, planning is an ongoing process that requires regular attention and adjustment. With the right mindset and tools, you can transform your plans into actions and your actions into success. While planning focus imparts us many things, one of the important things that we learn is the emergency planning process; as the name suggests, it prepares us for what we should be doing in case an emergency occurs; as they say in safety processes, missing or ignoring a certain number of near misses results in major incidents which then results in severe accidents. In planning processes too, failing or missing to plan frequently or not correcting the plan based on the progress can result in serious issues in the future. Hence, planning is the most essential skill one has to develop in life, and planning for your own aspirations is the key.

Planning isn't just about setting and achieving goals; it's about creating a clear path toward your desired future. It helps you make informed decisions, utilize your resources effectively, and adapt to changes with confidence. As you move forward, remember that the journey of planning is as important as the destination. Regularly review and update your plans, remain flexible, and be prepared to adjust your strategies as needed. With diligent planning, you can turn your aspirations into tangible accomplishments and enjoy a more organized, fulfilling life.

The person you will be in 5 years depends on:

- The food you eat
- Amount of exercise you do
- How much sleep per day
- Books or articles you read
- How much you write
- Money you save and invest
- Who you work with
- Friends you spend time with
- New skills you develop

– James Clear

"Success is the residue of planning."

– Benjamin Franklin

Planning worksheet :

What to plan

• work [professional; personal]

• aspiration

• Annual Calendar

• Quarterly

• Monthly

• Weekly

• Daily

• 5y plans

Area (don't forget to include Q2 focus areas) (3 to 5 areas)	Action (include timelines for completion)

Roughly right than precisely wrong

Notes

What did I learn?

What will I do differently?

ROUGHLY RIGHT RATHER THAN PRECISELY WRONG

Chapter 2
Time Management

On a daily basis, the effects of our actions are imperceptible; cumulatively, though, their consequences are enormous."

– Warren Buffett

Introduction

"Time isn't the main thing. It's the only thing."

– Stephen R. Covey

Time is precious and irreplaceable. Managing it well is key to leading a balanced and productive life. Whether it's work, family, or personal projects, how one handles time impacts everything. Effective time management helps us focus on what truly matters, achieve goals, and reduce stress. I often hear people say they don't have enough time. But I've realized that it's not about having time but about making time for what's important. It's all about making conscious choices and deciding what deserves my attention and energy. As Benjamin Franklin said, "Lost time is never found again." This reminder pushes me to use my time wisely.

Think about a typical day. If I spend the first few hours on minor tasks, I might not have enough time or energy for the essential projects. This is why prioritizing tasks is crucial. It ensures that the most critical tasks get done when my energy levels are high. Multitasking, which many of us pride ourselves on, is often counterproductive. It scatters my focus and reduces the quality of my work. By focusing on one task at a time and using techniques like Time-Blocking, I can enhance my productivity and reduce stress. Self-care is another vital aspect of time management. Just like a rechargeable battery, I need regular recharging; including relaxation and self-care in my schedule is not a luxury; it's a necessity. It keeps me energized and ready to tackle my tasks with a clear mind.

In this chapter, we'll explore practical techniques to help you make the most of each day. By learning how to prioritize tasks, avoid the pitfalls of multitasking, and incorporate self-care into your routine, you'll be better equipped to handle life's demands. With the right strategies, you can manage your time effectively and lead a more balanced and productive life.

Just as we learned about the core concepts of planning in Chapter 1, mastering time management also involves understanding some essential principles.

The Essence of Prioritization

When I think about prioritizing tasks, it's really about figuring out what needs my attention first. This way, I can make sure I'm spending my time on the things that matter most. For example, if I start my day with a long to-do list and no plan, I might waste time on less important tasks and miss the critical ones. By putting the most important tasks at the top of my list, I make sure I'm using my time wisely. Remember Benjamin Franklin's words: "Lost time is never found again." This always nudges me to focus on what's truly important.

Consider a typical workday. If you spend the first few hours on minor tasks, you might not have enough time or energy for essential projects. By prioritizing, you tackle the most critical tasks and address the key responsibilities when your energy levels are high. This approach ensures that you make the best use of your most productive hours. Effective prioritization involves evaluating tasks based on their importance and urgency. One helpful tool for this is the Eisenhower matrix, which categorizes tasks into four quadrants:

> "I have 2 kinds of problems, the urgent and the important. The urgent are not important, and the important are never urgent."
>
> **– Eisenhower**

1. Urgent and Important: These are tasks that need immediate attention and have significant consequences. They should be your top priority. For example, a pressing work deadline or a family emergency falls into this category.

2. Important but Not Urgent: These are tasks that are important but can be scheduled for later. Focus on these after addressing urgent tasks. Examples include long-term project planning or regular exercise routines.

3. Urgent but Not Important: These tasks require immediate action but are not crucial to your long-term goals. These can often be delegated. For instance, answering non-essential emails or attending certain meetings might fall here.

4. Neither Urgent Nor Important: Tasks that have little impact on your goals and can be minimized or eliminated. Scrolling through social media or other time-wasting activities often belong in this quadrant.

This method allows you to organize your tasks and focus on what truly matters. By regularly reviewing and adjusting your priorities, you can stay on track and make meaningful progress toward your goals.

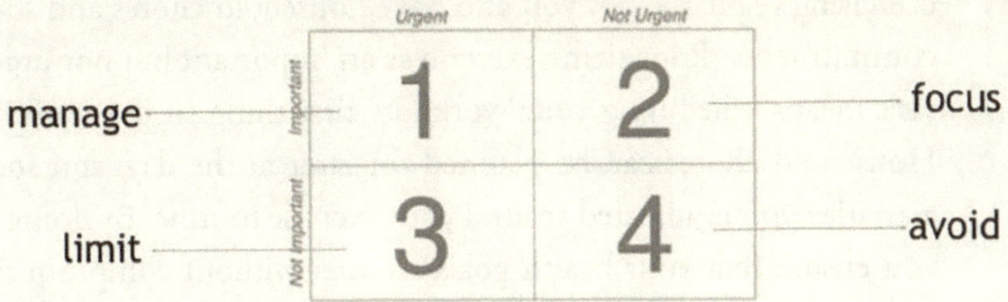

Prioritizing Tasks Offers Several Benefits Like:

- Improved Focus: You can concentrate on high-impact tasks without getting distracted by less important activities. This helps you stay on course and accomplish more.

- Increased Productivity: You make the best use of your time and energy by tackling the most important tasks first. This boosts your efficiency and ensures that critical tasks are completed.

- Reduced Stress: Knowing that you are addressing the most critical tasks can help reduce anxiety and create a sense of accomplishment. When you prioritize effectively, you feel more in control of your workload.

Let's look at some practical examples of how task prioritization can make a difference:

- Work Scenario: Imagine you are a project manager with a looming deadline for a major project. You also have several emails to answer and a team meeting to prepare for. By prioritizing, you focus first on completing the critical project tasks that directly impact the deadline. Emails can be addressed later, and the team meeting can be scheduled after the urgent project work is done. This approach ensures that the most crucial tasks are completed when your concentration and energy are at their peak.

- Personal Scenario: Suppose you want to improve your health by exercising regularly, but you also have household chores and social commitments. Prioritizing exercise as an important but not urgent task means scheduling your workouts first thing in the morning. Household chores can be planned for later in the day, and social activities can be adjusted around your exercise routine. By doing so, you ensure that your health goals are met without compromising other responsibilities. Several tools and techniques can help with task prioritization.

- To-Do Lists: A simple list of tasks, ranked by priority, can help keep you organized. Writing down tasks and ticking them off as you complete them provides a sense of accomplishment and keeps you focused on your goals.

- Time Blocking: Allocate specific time blocks in your calendar for high-priority tasks to ensure they get done. This method helps you dedicate uninterrupted time to important activities, increasing productivity and reducing the temptation to multitask.

- ABCDE Method: Rank tasks from A to E, with A being the most important and E the least. Focus on completing A tasks first. This technique helps you systematically address tasks based on their importance, ensuring that critical tasks are prioritized.

Key Takeaways

By mastering task prioritization, you can navigate your daily responsibilities more efficiently and achieve a balanced approach to both personal and professional life. As William Penn rightly said, "Time is what we want most, but what we use worst." By prioritizing wisely, you make the most of this invaluable resource. The next time you feel overwhelmed by your to-do list, take a moment to prioritize. Ask yourself which tasks are the most important and which can wait. Use tools like the Eisenhower Box to help you categorize tasks and focus on what truly matters. With practice, prioritization will become second nature, and you'll find yourself managing your time more effectively, reducing stress, and achieving your goals with greater ease.

Unveiling the Myth of Multitasking

Multitasking is often seen as a valuable skill, but in reality, it can be more harmful than helpful. Trying to do multiple tasks at once might seem efficient, but it often leads to mistakes and stress. Let's explore why focusing on one task at a time is more effective. But first, let's talk about the downside of multitasking.

Here are some specific drawbacks of multitasking:

1. Reduced Quality of Work: When I multitask, I find that the quality of my work suffers. Dividing attention between tasks means I'm not giving my best effort to any single task, which often leads to mistakes and subpar results. It's like trying to bake a cake while cooking a complex dish; both will likely turn out poorly.

2. Increased Errors: The likelihood of making mistakes increases with multitasking. Each time I switch tasks, my brain has to refocus, and this transition can cause errors. Important details can be overlooked, leading to costly mistakes, especially in tasks that require precision.

3. Slower Completion Times: Contrary to what many believe, multitasking can actually slow you down. Constantly shifting focus means it takes longer to complete each task compared to working on them sequentially. For example, writing an email while participating in a conference call often means neither is done effectively or efficiently.

4. Mental Exhaustion: Multitasking is mentally draining. Our brains use more energy to switch between tasks, leading to quicker

burnout. This mental fatigue can accumulate, making it harder to concentrate even on simpler tasks.

5. 5. Increased Stress Levels: The constant pressure to juggle multiple tasks can be overwhelming. Do you often feel stressed trying to keep up with everything at once? I do. This stress can affect both my mental and physical health over time.

The Benefits of Focusing on One Task at a Time

Focusing on one task at a time, also known as single-tasking, allows me to give my full attention to each activity. This approach improves the quality of my work and helps me complete tasks more quickly. When I concentrate on a single task, I can think more clearly and make fewer mistakes. Single-tasking also reduces stress. When I focus on one task, I feel more in control and less overwhelmed. Completing one task before moving on to the next gives me a sense of accomplishment and keeps my stress levels in check. It's like savoring one dish at a time during a meal instead of trying to eat everything at once.

Time Blocking: Allocating Specific Time Blocks for Focused Work

One effective way to practice single-tasking is through time-blocking. Have you ever tried to set specific times for different tasks? Time-blocking involves dedicating specific periods to different tasks throughout the day. By setting aside uninterrupted time for each task, I can focus better and get more done.

Here's how you can use time blocking:

1. Identify Your Tasks: List out everything you need to do for the day. This helps in visualizing all tasks and preparing mentally for the day ahead.

2. Set Priorities: Determine which tasks are most important and need your full attention. Ranking tasks helps you allocate the right amount of time for each.

3. Allocate Time Blocks: Assign specific time slots for each task. For example, dedicate 9-11 am for writing a report, 11-12 pm for answering emails, and so on. Make sure to include short breaks to rest and recharge.

4. Stick to Your Schedule: During each time block, focus solely on the task at hand. Avoid distractions like checking your phone or browsing the internet. If something urgent comes up, note it down and address it during its designated time.

Additional Tips for Successful Time Blocking

1. Buffer Time: Include buffer times between blocks to account for overruns and unexpected interruptions.

2. Review and Adjust: At the end of the day, review your time blocks and adjust for the next day based on what worked and what didn't.

3. Set Boundaries: Inform colleagues or family members of your time blocks to minimize interruptions.

4. Use Tools: Utilize tools like calendars or time-blocking apps to plan and track your schedule.

> "Instead of saying 'I don't have time' try saying 'it's not a priority,' and see how that feels."
>
> **– Laura Vanderkam**

Key Takeaways

Multitasking may appear efficient, but it usually causes errors and stress. Concentrating on one task at a time enhances productivity and lowers stress. Time-blocking is a powerful tool that helps you manage your time wisely and keep your focus on what's important. Creating a structured schedule allows you to concentrate on one task at a time. By practicing single-tasking and using time-blocking, you can manage your tasks better and achieve more with less stress.

Now that you know 2 of the core concepts, here are a few more that you can apply in your daily life once you master the first 2. These additional techniques will help you refine your time management skills and make the most of each day. By incorporating these practices, you can achieve a more balanced and productive life, reducing stress and increasing efficiency.

1. The Pomodoro Technique is a method I find incredibly effective for managing my time. This technique involves working in focused intervals, usually 25 minutes long, followed by a short break. By breaking my work into these manageable chunks, I can maintain high levels of concentration and prevent burnout. It's like giving my brain a mini recharge after each session, which keeps me productive throughout the day.

2. Carving out some 'me' time for self-care and relaxation is essential. Imagine trying to drive a car with an empty fuel tank. Without regular breaks and moments for yourself, it becomes difficult to keep going. Including self-care in your schedule ensures you remain energized and ready to handle your tasks. Whether it's a short walk, reading a book, or simply taking a few minutes to breathe deeply, these moments are vital for maintaining overall well-being.

3. Boosting productivity can be achieved with several techniques. One of my favorites is the Pareto Principle, also known as the 80/20 Rule. This principle suggests that 80% of our results

come from 20% of our efforts. By focusing on the tasks that have the most significant impact, I can make the best use of my time. Another useful technique is "Eating That Frog," which means tackling the most challenging task first thing in the morning. This approach not only boosts productivity but also gives a sense of accomplishment that motivates for the rest of the day.

4. Effective task scheduling and time allocation are crucial for staying organized. Planning the day and assigning specific time slots for each task helps me stay on track. Effective scheduling ensures that time is allocated appropriately, maximizing productivity. Sometimes it feels like the day slips away without getting much done. By having a clear plan, important tasks are completed on time, and there's no last-minute scrambling.

5. Using time tracking tools has been a game-changer. Time tracking and procrastination management go hand in hand. These tools help understand how time is spent and identify areas for improvement. By managing procrastination, accountability is enhanced, ensuring that goals are met. It's satisfying to see how much has been accomplished at the end of the day when focus is maintained and time is used wisely.

I've found that stories can be powerful in illustrating the importance of effective time management in real life. Let me share an anecdote about Leonardo da Vinci, which perfectly captures the concepts we've discussed so far. His mastery of time through balancing varied pursuits showcases the practical application of these principles and serves as an inspiring example of how to manage time effectively across different disciplines.

Leonardo da Vinci is often remembered as a genius who excelled in various fields—painting, anatomy, engineering, and more. But how did he manage to accomplish so much in one lifetime? The secret lies in his exceptional time management skills. Leonardo approached his day with a clear plan. He understood the importance of prioritization, often focusing on his most important tasks first. Whether it was working on a detailed sketch or conducting an anatomical study, he gave his full attention to each task, avoiding the pitfalls of multitasking. He knew that dividing his focus would dilute the quality of his work.

To maintain high levels of concentration, Leonardo used techniques similar to the Pomodoro Technique. He would work in intense, focused intervals, allowing himself short breaks in between. This method helped him stay productive and prevented burnout, enabling him to sustain his creative and intellectual output over long periods. Leonardo also recognized the necessity of self-care. He balanced his intense work sessions with moments of relaxation and reflection. This balance was crucial for maintaining his energy and creative flow. By taking care of his physical and mental well-being, he ensured that he could continue working effectively across his various interests.

One of the keys to Leonardo's success was his ability to use productivity techniques to his advantage. He was known for his meticulous to-do lists and detailed notes, which helped him keep track of his numerous projects. By scheduling his tasks and allocating specific time slots for each, he managed to stay organized and on top of his diverse endeavors. Moreover, Leonardo was a pioneer in using time tracking and accountability methods. He kept detailed journals where he recorded his progress, thoughts, and ideas. This habit not only helped him stay focused but also allowed him to reflect on his achievements and plan future projects more effectively.

To make it more relatable, imagine your own busy life. We often juggle work, family, and personal interests, just like Leonardo did. Think about how prioritizing your most important tasks first can set a positive tone for your day. Try working in focused intervals, and notice how your productivity and satisfaction improve. Remember to take breaks and care for yourself, ensuring you have the energy to keep going. Consider keeping a detailed to-do list or a journal. It doesn't have to be as elaborate as Leonardo's! But, noting down your tasks and progress can help you stay organized and motivated. Tracking your time and reflecting on your accomplishments can give you a sense of direction and purpose.

Leonardo da Vinci's ability to master time management and balance his varied pursuits is a testament to the power of the principles we've discussed. By prioritizing tasks, focusing intensely, taking care of himself, using productivity techniques, and tracking his progress, he achieved extraordinary success in multiple fields. His life serves as a powerful reminder that with the right time management strategies, we too can accomplish great things.

Let's look at another inspiring figure known for his exceptional time management: Benjamin Franklin. His daily schedule offers a historical example of how meticulous structuring can lead to productivity, personal growth, and rest. Benjamin Franklin was not only one of the Founding Fathers of the United States but also a prolific inventor, writer, and thinker. How did he manage to achieve so much in his lifetime? The secret lies in his disciplined approach to time management. Franklin's daily schedule was a testament to the power of planning and prioritization.

Franklin started his day with a simple yet profound question: "What good shall I do today?" This question set a positive tone for his day and aligned his actions with his goals. Starting the day with this intention helped him focus on what truly mattered. It's a great reminder for us to begin each day with a clear sense of purpose. His mornings were structured with time for personal growth. Franklin would spend the early hours reading, writing, and engaging in thoughtful reflection. This practice highlights the importance of dedicating time to self-improvement and lifelong learning. By investing in his personal growth, Franklin ensured that he was constantly evolving and expanding his knowledge.

Throughout the day, Franklin allocated specific time blocks for his various tasks. He had periods dedicated to work, meetings, and social interactions. By segmenting his day, he ensured that each activity received the attention it deserved without overwhelming his schedule. This method is akin to the time-blocking technique we discussed earlier. By breaking his day into smaller portions, Franklin could stay focused and productive. Franklin also understood the value of self-care. He included time for meals, rest, and relaxation in his daily schedule. By balancing his work with moments of rest, he maintained his energy and prevented burnout. This approach aligns with the concept of treating oneself like a rechargeable battery, ensuring you have the stamina to tackle each task effectively. Do you ever find yourself running on empty? Taking regular breaks, just as Franklin did, can help you recharge and stay productive.

In the evening, Franklin would review his day with another reflective question: "What good have I done today?" This practice allowed him to assess his accomplishments, learn from his experiences, and plan for the future. By tracking his progress and reflecting on his day, Franklin stayed accountable and continually improved his time management strategies. This evening reflection is a great way to end the day on a positive note and prepare for tomorrow. Franklin's meticulous scheduling demonstrates the power of structured time management. By planning his day, prioritizing tasks, dedicating time to personal growth, and ensuring regular self-care, he achieved a remarkable balance between productivity and rest. His approach serves as a timeless example of how effective time management can lead to a fulfilling and successful life.

Reflecting on Franklin's schedule, consider how you can incorporate similar practices into your own life. Start your day with a question that sets a positive intention, allocate specific time blocks for your tasks, and remember to include moments for personal growth and self-care. By doing so, you can create a balanced and productive routine that helps you achieve your goals and maintain your well-being.

The sheet that Franklin used

The morning question, What good shall I do this day?	5	Rise, wash, and address *Powerful Goodness;* contrive day's business and take the resolution of the day; prosecute the present study; and breakfast.
	6	
	7	
	8	
	9	Work.
	10	
	11	
	12	Read or overlook my accounts, and dine.
	1	
	2	Work.
	3	
	4	
	5	
	6	Put things in their places, supper, music, or diversion, or conversation; examination of the day.
	7	
	8	
	9	
Evening question, What good have I done today?	10	
	11	
	12	
	1	Sleep.
	2	
	3	
	4	

Source : The autobiography of Benjamin Franklin

Let's dive into another story that vividly illustrates the importance of prioritizing significant tasks: the professor's demonstration with jars, rocks, pebbles, and sand. This simple yet powerful visual can help you understand how to manage your time more efficiently.

Imagine a professor standing in front of his class with an empty glass jar. He begins by filling the jar with large rocks. These rocks represent the most important tasks and priorities in your life, such as family, health, and significant work projects. The professor then asks the students if the jar is full. They agree it is. Next, he adds small pebbles into the jar, shaking it slightly so the pebbles fill the spaces between the rocks. These pebbles symbolize other important tasks that are not as crucial as the rocks but still matter, like work deadlines and personal commitments. Again, he asks the students if the jar is full. They agree it is.

Finally, the professor pours sand into the jar. The sand fills the remaining spaces, representing the small, everyday tasks and distractions that can fill up our time but don't add much value. Once more, he asks if the jar is full, and the students respond affirmatively. The professor explains that the jar represents your life. If you fill your jar with sand first, there will be no room left for the rocks and pebbles. This is what happens when you spend too much time on minor tasks and distractions. But if you place the rocks first, then the pebbles, and finally the sand, everything fits perfectly. This demonstrates the importance of prioritizing your significant tasks first. By focusing on what truly matters, you can ensure that the most important aspects of your life are addressed, and the smaller tasks will naturally find their place.

What about your own daily routine? Are you filling your jar with sand, leaving little room for the big rocks? Or are you focusing on the important tasks first, ensuring that you manage your time effectively?

When I reflect on this demonstration, it reminds me to evaluate how I allocate my time. Am I prioritizing the big rocks in my life? Starting the day by identifying the most important tasks and scheduling them first has made a significant difference in how I manage my time. This approach ensures that I address what truly matters, and the smaller tasks fit in around them. Imagine your schedule as the jar. Place your big rocks—your most important tasks—first. Then, add the pebbles, the other important tasks, and let the sand, the small daily tasks, fill in the gaps. This way, you ensure that your life is balanced and that your most critical responsibilities are not overshadowed by less important activities.

This story is a powerful reminder to prioritize what matters most. By focusing on the big rocks first, you'll find that you have more time and energy for the things that truly make a difference in your life. It's a simple yet profound way to approach time management, ensuring that you live a balanced and fulfilling life. So, the next time you plan your day, ask yourself: what are my big rocks? Start with those, and let everything else fall into place. This strategy will help you manage your time more efficiently and achieve a better balance between work, personal commitments, and relaxation. By keeping the image of the jar, rocks, pebbles, and sand in mind, you can remind yourself to focus on what truly matters and make the most of your time.

Effective time management relies not just on understanding the core concepts but also on using the right tools and techniques to put these concepts into practice. By integrating these tools into your daily routine, you can streamline your tasks, stay focused, and make the most out of every moment. Let's explore some key tools and techniques that can help you manage your time more efficiently and achieve your goals with greater ease.

As discussed earlier in the chapter, the Eisenhower Matrix is a powerful tool for time management. This simple yet effective technique helps categorize tasks based on their urgency and importance, making it easier to decide what needs immediate attention and what can be scheduled for later.

The Eisenhower Matrix, named after President Dwight D. Eisenhower, divides tasks into 4 quadrants:

1. Urgent and Important

2. Important but Not Urgent

3. Urgent but Not Important

4. Neither Urgent Nor Important

Let's break it down further with an example. Picture this: you have a busy workday ahead. Begin by writing down all your tasks and then sorting them into the right categories. Here's a practical example - you need to prepare for an important presentation at work.

Quadrant 1: Urgent and Important

- Completing a project with a tight deadline

- Addressing an urgent client request

Quadrant 2: Important but Not Urgent

- Planning next month's marketing strategy

- Enrolling in a course to improve your skills

Quadrant 3: Urgent but Not Important

- Responding to a non-critical email

- Attending an impromptu meeting that doesn't require your input

Quadrant 4: Neither Urgent Nor Important

- Browsing social media

- Organizing files that don't need immediate attention

By categorizing your tasks in this way, you can see at a glance what needs your immediate focus and what can wait. This helps in preventing the feeling of being overwhelmed and ensures that your time is spent on activities that truly matter.

Here's how you can implement the Eisenhower Matrix in your daily routine:

1. List Your Tasks: Start by writing down everything you need to do. Don't worry about the order or priority at this stage—just get everything out of your head and onto paper.

2. Categorize: Place each task into one of the four quadrants based on its urgency and importance.

3. Prioritize: Focus on Quadrant 1 tasks first. These are your immediate priorities. Next, allocate time for Quadrant 2 tasks, as these are crucial for long-term success. Try to delegate or minimize Quadrant 3 tasks and eliminate Quadrant 4 tasks where possible.

4. Review Regularly: Make this a regular practice. At the start of each day or week, take a few minutes to review and update your matrix. This ensures that you stay on top of your priorities and adjust as needed.

Using the Eisenhower Matrix helps you stay organized and focused, making sure that your efforts align with your most important goals. It's a straightforward tool that can have a profound impact on how you manage your time. By visualizing your tasks and understanding their priority, you can navigate your day with more clarity and purpose. Give it a try and see how it transforms your productivity and reduces stress.

Another powerful tool that we spoke about for effective time management is the Pareto Principle, also known as the 80/20 Rule. This principle suggests that 80% of your results come from 20% of your efforts. By focusing on the tasks that offer the most significant rewards, you can maximize productivity and achieve your goals more efficiently. The Pareto Principle is named after Italian economist Vilfredo Pareto, who observed that 80% of Italy's wealth was owned by 20% of the population. This principle can be applied to various aspects of life, including time management. It's all about identifying and prioritizing the tasks that have the greatest impact.

Let's explore how you can use the Pareto Principle in your daily routine

Identifying High-Impact Tasks

Start by listing all your tasks and responsibilities. Then, analyze which tasks contribute the most to your goals. These are your high-impact tasks—the 20% that produce 80% of your results. It might be a major project at work, key client meetings, or essential personal commitments. For example, if you're a sales manager, you might find that most of your revenue comes from a handful of key clients. In this case, focusing on nurturing these relationships and closing deals with these clients would be your high-impact tasks.

Prioritizing High-Impact Tasks

Once you've identified your high-impact tasks, prioritize them. Allocate more time and resources to these tasks, ensuring they are completed to the best of your ability. This doesn't mean you should neglect other tasks, but the bulk of your focus should be on what brings the most value. Imagine you have a list of 10 tasks for the day. According to the Pareto Principle, 2 of these tasks will likely account for most of your productivity. By completing these first, you ensure that your most important work is done, and the rest of the day can be spent on less critical activities.

Let's put this into a real-life scenario. Suppose you're preparing for a major presentation at work. The high-impact tasks might include researching key data, creating a compelling narrative, and practicing your delivery. These tasks are crucial to the success of your presentation and should be your primary focus. On the other hand, tasks like organizing your desk or checking emails, while still important, don't significantly contribute to the success of your presentation. By applying the Pareto Principle, you would spend most of your time on the high-impact tasks, ensuring your presentation is well-prepared and effective.

The Pareto Principle isn't a one-time exercise. Regularly evaluate your tasks and priorities to ensure you're always focusing on what matters most. This might involve weekly reviews of your goals and the tasks that contribute most to them. Adjust your focus as needed to stay aligned with your priorities. One of the challenges in applying the Pareto Principle is staying focused on high-impact tasks and avoiding distractions. It's easy to get caught up in low-impact activities that consume your time but offer little reward. Be mindful of this and create strategies to minimize distractions. This could be setting specific times for checking emails or limiting time spent on non-essential activities.

The Pareto Principle isn't just for work; it can be applied to your personal life too. What are the activities that bring you the most joy and fulfillment? It might be spending quality time with family, pursuing a hobby, or taking care of your health. Focus on these high-impact activities to enhance your overall well-being. For instance, if you find that 20% of your social interactions bring you 80% of your happiness, prioritize spending time with those key people. Similarly, if certain exercises yield the best results for your fitness, focus more on those workouts.

By identifying and prioritizing high-impact tasks, you can make the most of your time and achieve your goals more efficiently by using the Pareto Principle. Regularly applying this principle ensures that your efforts are aligned with your most significant outcomes, both in your professional and personal life. Next time you plan your day, remember the 80/20 Rule. Focus on the tasks that will make the biggest difference, and watch how your productivity and satisfaction improve. It's a simple yet transformative approach to time management that can lead to significant rewards.

Another powerful technique for managing time effectively and boosting productivity is the concept known as "Eat That Frog." This idea, popularized by Brian Tracy, is all about tackling the most challenging tasks first. By getting the toughest task out of the way early, you can set a positive tone for the rest of your day and significantly boost both productivity and morale. The phrase "Eat That Frog" comes from a famous quote by Mark Twain: "If it's your job to eat a frog, it's best to do it first thing in the morning. And if it's your job to eat 2 frogs, it's best to eat the biggest one first." The frog represents your most daunting task—the one you're most likely to procrastinate on but that also has the most significant impact on your day.

Why Tackle the Toughest Task First?

Starting your day by tackling the most challenging task has several benefits:

1. Boosts Productivity: By completing the hardest task first, you create a sense of accomplishment that can carry you through the rest of the day. It makes the remaining tasks seem easier in comparison.

2. Reduces Procrastination: Getting the toughest task out of the way reduces the temptation to procrastinate. Once the biggest hurdle is cleared, you'll find it easier to stay focused and motivated.

3. Increases Morale: Successfully handling a difficult task first thing in the morning gives you a confidence boost and sets a positive tone for the day. This can improve your overall mood and outlook.

To effectively apply this technique, you first need to identify your "frog." Ask yourself: what is the most important task I need to complete today? Which task will have the most significant impact on my goals? It might be a critical work project, an important decision you've been putting off, or a challenging personal task.

Implementing "Eat That Frog" in Your Routine

1. Start with Planning: At the end of each day or the beginning of the next, take a few minutes to list your tasks and identify your "frog." Make this task your top priority for the day.

2. Tackle It First: Begin your day by focusing on your most challenging task. Avoid distractions and commit to working on it until it's completed. This may require you to block out specific times in your schedule dedicated solely to this task.

3. Break It Down: If the task is too large or overwhelming, break it down into smaller, more manageable steps. This way, you can tackle each step one at a time, making the overall task less daunting.

4. Stay Committed: It's easy to get sidetracked or tempted to push the task to later in the day. Stay committed to the principle of "eating that frog" first. Remind yourself of the benefits and push through any initial resistance.

Try recalling a time when you had a significant task that you kept putting off. How did it feel once you finally completed it? The relief and sense of accomplishment likely outweighed the initial dread. By consistently applying the "Eat That Frog" technique, you can transform how you approach your day and manage your workload.

Let's say you have a major report due at work, and it's been hanging over your head for days. Instead of starting your day with smaller tasks like checking emails or attending meetings, you decide to tackle the report first. You block out the first 2 hours of your morning, eliminate distractions, and dive into the report. By the time you finish, you feel a sense of achievement and relief. The rest of your tasks for the day seem much more manageable, and you can approach them with a clear mind and higher energy. Consistently applying the "Eat That Frog" technique can lead to long-term benefits. It helps build discipline and reduces the habit of procrastination. Over time, you'll find that you're able to take on challenging tasks with more confidence and less hesitation. This not only improves your productivity but also enhances your overall effectiveness and success.

The "Eat That Frog" technique is a straightforward yet highly effective approach to time management. By tackling your most challenging tasks first, you can boost productivity, reduce procrastination, and enhance your morale. Start incorporating this technique into your daily routine and experience the transformative impact it can have on your productivity and overall satisfaction. The hardest part is taking the first bite, but the rewards are well worth it.

One must also be aware of an important concept, Parkinson's law:

Basically, it says that work expands to fill the time available for its completion, it explains as how tasks tend to take up all the time allotted for their completion, even if they could be finished sooner.

This principle sheds light on the ineffeciencies of time management, procrastination, and over complication of task.

Key concepts

Perceived time vs actual need :'If a task is given one week, it will often expand in complexity or detail to fill the entire week, even if it could be done in two days

Time and effort are not proportional :Just because more time is spent on a task doesn't necessarily mean better results. Extra time can lead to overthinking, unnecessary refinements or distractions

Human tendency toward procrastination:

Withour clear deadline, people naturally delay starting or completing a task, stretching it unnecessarily

'If you wait until the last minute, it only takes a minute to do"

> "Small steps matter more when you play a long game because a long horizon allows you to compound small advances into quite large achievements."
>
> **– Kevin Kelly**

Final thoughts

Mastering time management isn't just about ticking off tasks on a to-do list; it's about creating a lifestyle that allows you to take control of your time and, ultimately, your destiny. By learning and applying the techniques we've discussed—prioritizing tasks, focusing on one thing at a time, and incorporating self-care—you can transform how you approach your days. Think about Leonardo da Vinci and Benjamin Franklin, whose disciplined approaches to time management allowed them to achieve remarkable things in various fields. Remember the story of the professor with the jars, rocks, pebbles, and sand, illustrating the importance of prioritizing significant tasks first. These anecdotes aren't just interesting tales; they offer practical wisdom that can be applied to our everyday lives.

The Eisenhower Matrix helps us sort through the chaos by distinguishing urgent tasks from important ones. The Pareto Principle guides us to focus on the 20% of efforts that yield 80% of results, ensuring we make the most impactful use of our time. The "Eat That Frog" technique encourages us to tackle the toughest tasks first, boosting our productivity and morale from the get-go. Incorporating these strategies, among several others that are easy to understand, into your routine can help you achieve a more balanced and productive life. It's not about cramming more into your day; it's about making more meaningful choices with your time. Effective time management allows you to focus on what truly matters, reducing stress and increasing satisfaction.

As you move forward, keep in mind that these techniques are tools to help you manage your time better and reach your goals. They are not rigid rules but flexible guidelines that you can adapt to fit your unique needs and circumstances. Take the principles we've discussed and integrate them into your daily life. Reflect on your goals, prioritize your tasks, focus on what matters most, and don't forget to make time for yourself. By doing so, you'll find that you can handle life's demands with greater ease and enjoy a more fulfilling and balanced life.

Time is your most valuable resource. Use it wisely, and you'll find that you have more of it for the things that truly matter. With effective time management, you can shape your destiny and live a life that is both productive and satisfying.

Psychotherapist and author Charles Richardson on productivity:

"Don't be fooled by the calendar. There are only as many days in the year as you make use of. One person gets only a week's value out of a year while another gets a full year's value out of a week."

"What you do on a daily basis, even imperfectly done, will give you far greater results than what you can do perfectly but do on a irregular basis."

– TT Rangarajan

Laziness Index

How to measure your laziness:

- Every time you tell yourself to do something, count that as a task (what you tell yourself, no external force)

- Every time you accomplish the task, give yourself 1 mark (even if the task is not completed but initiated, you will still get 1 mark)

- Every time you either don't initiate or complete the task, you will get zero marks.

- Before going to bed, evaluate your score: completed/initiated tasks minus total tasks.

- As long as the score is positive, you are ok; however, if the score negative, rethink your tasks and be aware.

- The advantage of this approach is that you do not complain or blame others or any other external system.

- It's you who assigned tasks; no one ever forced you.

> "Impracticality is the vocabulary of a mediocre who doesn't want to take the responsibility of implementation."
>
> – TT Rangarajan

NOTES

What did I learn?

`

`

`

`

`

What will I do differently?

`

`

`

`

`

Chapter 3
Communication

"In conversations, listening is very important. In public speaking, expression and clarity of thought are very important. In your day-to-day dealings with others, listening is more important, and communicating with clarity is very important."

– Madhusudan

Introduction

"The single biggest problem in communication is the illusion that it has taken place."

– George Bernard Shaw

Communication is the cornerstone of any relationship, be it personal or professional. It's a skill that, if mastered, can open doors, resolve conflicts, and build strong connections. But we often fall into the trap of assuming that our messages are clear and that our words are understood exactly as we intended. This assumption can lead to misunderstandings and conflicts that shouldn't have come up in the first place. From my years of experience, both in the workplace and in personal relationships, I've learned that effective communication is not just about speaking or writing. It's mainly about engaging with others in a way that they can understand and respond to. It's about being present, listening actively, and also showing empathy. Communication isn't just about exchanging information; it's about the deeper connections that you form with people.

Clear communication is critical for teamwork and collaboration in our professional lives. It helps projects move forward smoothly, ensures everyone is on the same page, and prevents critical errors. In personal relationships, it builds trust and intimacy. Miscommunications, no matter how small, can snowball into bigger issues if not addressed promptly and clearly. When was the last time you had a misunderstanding with someone? Chances are, it wasn't because of the words themselves, but rather because of the assumptions behind said words. Maybe you assumed they understood your point, or they assumed you meant something else altogether. These seemingly small gaps in understanding can create significant problems.

That's why it's so important to maintain clarity about how we communicate. We need to ensure that our messages are clear, that we are truly listening to the other person, and most importantly, that we are aware of the nonverbal cues we are sending. Communication is not just about the words we speak, but also about how we use them, the tone of our voice, our body language, and our ability to listen and understand the perspectives of others who are involved in the conversation. We'll delve into various aspects that make communication effective as we explore the core concepts of communication in this chapter. We'll look at active listening, the power of empathy, the importance of nonverbal communication, and the need for clarity and conciseness. We'll also explore techniques for modifying our communication according to different audiences and the critical role of feedback in personal and professional growth.

Communication is one of the most important traits that distinguish human beings from other creatures. While many of us take it for granted, believing it simply involves speaking in a familiar language, true communication is not about being talkative or impressing others with our words. Rather, it is fundamentally about listening. Mastering the art of listening enhances our communication skills, as being fully aware and attentive allows for more meaningful interactions. When we speak, we are often in a rush to express our thoughts or eagerly anticipate our turn to respond. This hinders genuine communication.

This chapter also emphasizes the importance of listening skills, as well as the concepts of attention, concentration, and focus. We tend to admire individuals who articulate well, particularly in public settings, but the key to their effective communication lies in their habits of extensive reading and attentive listening. Good communicators read a lot, which fuels their creativity and equips them to share their thoughts lucidly. Equally important is their ability to listen attentively and respond thoughtfully, ensuring their communication is apt and impactful. Without these skills, it is challenging to be an effective communicator. Mastering the skill of listening is crucial for those aspiring to excel in their careers, entrepreneurial ventures, or personal relationships.

This skill, though difficult to practice, sets one apart and helps build strong connections with others. Recognizing our own listening deficiencies is the first step toward mastering this essential skill, leading to more profound and effective communication. Communication requires continuous practice and refinement. It's not something we can perfect overnight, but by understanding and applying the principles we'll discuss in this chapter, we can significantly improve our ability to connect with others while building stronger, more meaningful relationships.

1. Active Listening and Empathetic Communication

Communication isn't just about speaking; it's equally about listening. I've come to understand that truly listening to someone is like appreciating each note in a symphony. It requires full engagement and an open heart. Active listening is a skill that can transform our interactions, making the other person feel heard and valued. Imagine sitting in a concert hall, the orchestra playing a beautiful piece. To fully appreciate the music, you need to be present, attentive to each instrument, and the harmonies they create together. Similarly, in conversations, active listening means being fully present, not just hearing the words but understanding the emotions and intentions behind them. It's about paying attention to the speaker, making eye contact, and responding appropriately to show that you are truly engaged.

One of the most significant aspects of active listening is empathy. Empathy goes beyond mere understanding; it's about feeling what the other person feels. When you listen with empathy, you connect on a deeper emotional level. This connection fosters trust and openness, essential ingredients for effective communication. Let me share a personal experience. A few years ago, a close friend was going through a tough time. I remember sitting with him, listening to his frustrations and worries. Instead of jumping in with advice or solutions, I focused on understanding his feelings. I nodded, maintained eye contact, and occasionally repeated back what he said to ensure I got it right. This simple act of empathetic listening made a significant difference. He later told me that just having someone who genuinely listened made him feel supported and less alone.

Empathetic communication isn't always easy. It requires us to step outside our own experiences and put ourselves in someone else's shoes. It's about suspending judgment and being open to their perspective, even if it differs from our own. This openness can transform how we interact with others, making our communication more meaningful and effective. Think about the last time you felt truly heard. How did it make you feel? Probably valued, understood, and connected. That's the power of active listening and empathy. These skills are vital not just in personal relationships but also in professional settings. A manager who listens empathetically to their team can build stronger relationships, foster a supportive work environment, and drive better performance.

Empathetic communication helps us navigate difficult conversations and resolve conflicts more effectively. When we listen with empathy, we acknowledge the other person's feelings and perspectives, which can de-escalate tensions and pave the way for finding common ground. Incorporating active listening and empathy into our daily interactions can be transformative. Being present is crucial, so put away distractions like your phone or computer and focus entirely on the person you're communicating with. Maintain eye contact to show you're engaged and interested in what they're saying. Reflect and clarify by repeating back what you've heard in your own words to confirm understanding, and ask questions if something isn't clear. Show empathy by acknowledging their feelings and validating their experiences with phrases like "I understand how you feel" or "That sounds really tough." Finally, avoid interrupting and let them finish their thoughts without jumping in, as sometimes just letting someone talk can be incredibly therapeutic for them.

Communication is a two-way street. It's not just about getting our message across but also about understanding others. By practicing active listening and empathetic communication, we can build stronger, more meaningful relationships, both personally and professionally.

Key Takeaways

Active listening and empathetic communication are foundational to building strong, meaningful relationships. Fully engaging with others by giving them our undivided attention and appreciating each nuance of their message, much like savoring each note in a symphony, enhances understanding and connection. Empathy, in turn, allows us to connect on a deeper emotional level, making others feel heard and valued. By practicing these skills, we can improve our interactions, reduce misunderstandings, and foster a sense of mutual respect and trust in both personal and professional relationships.

2. Non-verbal Communication

Communication goes far beyond the words we speak. In fact, much of what we convey to others is through nonverbal cues—our body language, facial expressions, gestures, and even the tone of our voice. It's fascinating how much we can say without uttering a single word. Nonverbal communication is like the expressive movements of a dance, where each gesture and posture tells a part of the story. Consider a conversation where you're sharing exciting news with a friend. If they sit with their arms crossed and avoid eye contact, no matter how supportive their words might be, their body language could suggest disinterest or discomfort. Conversely, someone leaning forward, nodding, and maintaining eye contact conveys engagement and enthusiasm, even if they haven't said much. This is the power of nonverbal communication—it adds depth and context to our interactions.

From my own experiences, I've realized how important it is to be aware of these nonverbal signals. Years ago, I worked with a colleague who was excellent at his job but often seemed unapproachable because of his body language. He would sit with his arms crossed and rarely smiled during meetings, which unintentionally created a barrier between him and the rest of the team. It wasn't until he became aware of this and started adopting more open body language—uncrossing his arms, smiling more, and maintaining better eye contact—that his interactions with the team improved significantly.

Nonverbal cues can significantly impact the message we are trying to convey. Imagine trying to comfort someone who is upset. Your words might be soothing, but if your tone is flat and your arms are rigid by your sides, your message may not come across as intended. On the other hand, a warm tone, a gentle touch on the shoulder, and an open, relaxed posture can communicate empathy and support far more effectively. Body language can also help us gauge the truthfulness and intentions of others. We've all heard the phrase "actions speak louder than words," and in many cases, this rings true. For example, when someone says they agree with you but avoids eye contact and shifts uncomfortably, it's likely that their words don't match their true feelings. Being attuned to these discrepancies can help us navigate conversations more effectively and understand the underlying emotions and intentions of those we communicate with.

In a professional setting, mastering nonverbal communication can enhance leadership and teamwork. Leaders who display confident body language—standing tall, making eye contact, and using purposeful gestures—can inspire and motivate their teams more effectively. Similarly, team members who use positive nonverbal cues can foster a more collaborative and supportive work environment. Nonverbal communication is also crucial in cross-cultural interactions. Different cultures have varying interpretations of body language and gestures. For instance, maintaining eye contact is seen as a sign of confidence and honesty in some cultures, while in others, it can be perceived as disrespectful or confrontational. Understanding these cultural differences is essential for effective communication in our increasingly globalized world.

It's not just about being aware of others' nonverbal cues; it's also about being mindful of our own. Reflect on your own body language during conversations. Do you appear open and engaged, or do you inadvertently send signals of disinterest or tension? Small adjustments, like uncrossing your arms, nodding while listening, and smiling genuinely, can make a big difference in how others perceive you and how your messages are received. Improving nonverbal communication takes conscious effort and practice. Here are some strategies to help you become more adept at reading and conveying nonverbal signals:

1. **Self-Awareness:** Start by becoming more aware of your own body language. Pay attention to your posture, gestures, and facial expressions in different situations. Notice how people respond to you and adjust your nonverbal cues accordingly.

2. **Mirror Others:** When appropriate, subtly mirroring the body language of the person you're speaking with can create a sense of rapport and understanding. This doesn't mean copying them exactly, but adopting similar gestures or posture can signal that you're engaged and empathetic.

3. **Observe and Learn:** Watch how effective communicators use their body language. Notice how they stand, the gestures they use, and their facial expressions. Try to incorporate some of these positive non-verbal cues into your own interactions.

4. **Practice Eye Contact:** Eye contact is one of the most powerful nonverbal cues. It shows confidence and attentiveness. Practice maintaining eye contact during conversations, but be mindful not to stare, as it can make people uncomfortable.

5. **Use Gestures Purposefully:** Gestures can emphasise your words and help convey your message more effectively. Use your hands

to illustrate points, but ensure your gestures are natural and not exaggerated.

6. **Facial Expressions Matter:** Your facial expressions should match the content and tone of your message. A smile can be encouraging, while a serious expression can convey the gravity of a situation. Practice making your facial expressions more intentional.

7. **Mind Your Tone:** The tone of your voice can greatly influence how your message is received. Practice varying your pitch and volume to keep your audience engaged and to emphasize key points.

8. **Give and Receive Feedback:** Don't hesitate to ask trusted friends or colleagues for feedback on your nonverbal communication. They can provide valuable insights into how you come across and suggest areas for improvement.

9. **Relax and Be Natural:** Non-verbal communication should feel natural and not forced. Practice relaxing your body and letting your gestures flow naturally during conversations. The more comfortable you are, the more genuine and effective your non-verbal cues will be.

To sum up, non-verbal communication is a powerful tool that complements our verbal interactions. It adds layers of meaning and emotion to our words, helping us connect more deeply and authentically with others. Just like in a dance, where every movement conveys a part of the story, our non-verbal cues play a crucial role in the narrative of our communication. By becoming more aware of these cues and using them intentionally, we can improve our interactions and build stronger, more meaningful relationships.

> "Good communication is the bridge between confusion and clarity."
>
> **– Nat Turner**

Key Takeaways

Nonverbal communication is a powerful and often overlooked aspect of how we convey our thoughts and emotions. It goes beyond words, encompassing body language, facial expressions, gestures, and tone of voice. Being aware of these nonverbal cues can significantly enhance our interactions, making them more authentic and impactful. Improving nonverbal communication involves becoming more self-aware, practicing positive body language, observing effective communicators, and being mindful of cultural differences. By consciously working on these aspects, we can connect more deeply with others, ensure our messages are received as intended, and build stronger, more meaningful relationships both personally and professionally.

1. Assertive Communication and Conflict Resolution

Assertive communication is key to balancing our needs with those of others, much like finding a middle path that respects everyone involved. When we communicate assertively, we express our thoughts and feelings honestly and respectfully, without being aggressive or passive. This approach helps in resolving conflicts effectively by fostering an environment of mutual respect and understanding. It allows us to stand up for ourselves while also valuing the perspectives of others, leading to more productive and harmonious interactions.

2. Tailoring Communication to Different Audiences

Adapting our communication style to suit different audiences is crucial for ensuring our message is understood and effective. Just as a chef adjusts recipes to cater to various tastes, we need to modify our language, tone, and approach based on who we are speaking to. Whether we're talking to a colleague, a friend, or a family member, understanding their background, expectations, and communication preferences can make a significant difference in how our message is received and acted upon.

3. Verbal Communication

The words we choose, our tone, and how clearly we articulate our thoughts play a vital role in verbal communication. It's not just about what we say, but how we say it. Clear, precise language helps avoid misunderstandings and ensures that our message is conveyed effectively. Paying attention to our tone can also add the right emotional context to our words, whether we're offering support, giving instructions, or sharing ideas. Remember, as Peter Drucker said, "The most important thing in communication is hearing what isn't said."

4. Clarity and Conciseness

Being clear and concise is essential for effective communication. When we eliminate unnecessary words and get straight to the point, our message is easier to understand and more impactful. This approach not only saves time but also reduces the likelihood of confusion and errors. Striving for clarity and brevity helps ensure that our communication is direct and meaningful, making it more likely that our message will be received as intended.

5. Empathy

Empathy in communication involves understanding and sharing the feelings of others. It's about putting ourselves in their shoes and seeing the world from their perspective. This emotional connection can greatly enhance our interactions, making others feel heard and valued. Empathy builds trust and strengthens relationships, both personally and professionally. It allows us to respond more thoughtfully and supportively, creating a more compassionate and collaborative environment.

6. Feedback

Giving and receiving feedback is a critical tool for improving communication and fostering growth. Constructive feedback helps us understand our strengths and areas for improvement, guiding us toward better performance and stronger relationships. When offering feedback, it's important to be specific, respectful, and focused on behaviors rather than personal traits. Receiving feedback with an open mind and a willingness to learn can lead to significant personal and professional development. As John Powell wisely said, "Communication works for those who work at it."

The Butterfly Effect of Miscommunication

Miscommunication is like a small pebble causing ripples across a calm lake, and sometimes those ripples can turn into waves. Let's consider an example to understand this better. Imagine a scenario in a bustling corporate office where a team is preparing for a crucial client presentation. The team leader sends out an email with detailed instructions, assigning each team member specific sections to prepare. It seems straightforward, but a minor misunderstanding turns what should have been a smooth process into a series of escalating issues.

One of the team members, let's call him Raj, misunderstands his assignment. He thinks he is supposed to prepare the introduction, while in reality, he is assigned the conclusion. As the day of the presentation approaches, everyone works diligently on their parts, oblivious to the mix-up. It isn't until the night before the big day that the error is discovered. Raj has spent hours crafting a detailed introduction, and nobody has prepared the conclusion. This small miscommunication throws the team into a frenzy. The night before the presentation, the team realizes the oversight. The panic sets in as they scramble to put together a coherent conclusion at the last minute. Each team member is already stretched thin with their own sections, but they have no choice but to pull an all-nighter to fix the problem. The stress is palpable, and the atmosphere is tense. Everyone pitches in, trying to salvage the situation. However, the lack of preparation time for the conclusion is evident, and the final product is not as polished as it could have been.

The day of the presentation arrives, and the team steps into the conference room with the client. They start the presentation, and while the introduction is solid, the hastily prepared conclusion lacks depth and cohesion. The client notices the discrepancy and starts to question the team's professionalism and attention to detail. The impact of that one small miscommunication is now glaringly apparent. What was supposed to be a seamless presentation ends up feeling disjointed and underwhelming. After the presentation, the team reflects on what went wrong. They realize that a simple check-in or a confirmation email could have prevented the whole fiasco. This experience becomes a learning moment for the team. They understand that effective communication is not just about sending a message but ensuring that the message is received and understood correctly. They start implementing regular check-ins and confirmations to avoid such issues in the future.

This scenario illustrates how something as small as a misinterpreted email can lead to major problems. It underscores the necessity of ensuring our messages are clear and confirming understanding. Simple steps like asking for feedback or a quick acknowledgment can prevent such misunderstandings. Effective communication is the foundation of successful relationships, whether personal or professional. Just as a solid foundation is crucial for a sturdy building, clear and precise communication is essential for smooth operations and positive outcomes. This anecdote reminds us that even small details matter and taking the time to communicate effectively can save a lot of trouble down the road. The lesson here is that clear communication is more than just exchanging information; it's about making sure that what you intend to convey is what the other person understands. Miscommunications, even minor ones, can snowball into significant issues if not addressed promptly. By being vigilant and proactive in our communication, we can prevent misunderstandings and ensure that our interactions are productive and effective.

Key Tools and Techniques

To truly excel in communication, it's essential to understand and utilize a variety of tools and techniques that can enhance our interactions. In this section, we will delve into several key models and methods that provide a deeper understanding of communication dynamics. By exploring the Four-Sides Model of Communication, Nonviolent Communication, and Reflective Listening, we will gain valuable insights and practical strategies to improve our ability to connect with others effectively.

Four-Sides Model of Communication

The Four-Sides Model, developed by Friedemann Schulz von Thun, illustrates that every message has 4 dimensions: factual information, self-revelation, relationship, and appeal. Understanding these dimensions can lead to more effective interactions:

1. **Factual Information:** This is the content or the factual data that the message contains. It answers the question, "What is being

talked about?" For example, if someone says, "The meeting starts at 10 AM," the factual information is the start time of the meeting.

2. **Self-Revelation:** This dimension reveals something about the sender. It provides insight into the sender's feelings, motives, or personality, answering, "What does this say about me?" For instance, when a colleague mentions, "I'm swamped with tasks," it reveals their state of being overwhelmed.

3. **Relationship:** This aspect reflects the relationship between the sender and the receiver, indicating how the sender views the receiver. It answers, "What do I think of you?" For example, saying, "You're always late," not only addresses the punctuality issue but also implies a judgment about the receiver's habits.s habits.

4. **Appeal:** This is the sender's request or demand directed at the receiver, asking, "What do I want you to do?" For instance, "Please finish the report by tomorrow," is a clear appeal for action.

By recognizing these dimensions, we can better understand the full scope of a message and respond more appropriately. For example, if a colleague says, "The report needs to be done by tomorrow," we should consider the factual content (the deadline), the self-revelation (perhaps the colleague is stressed), the relationship (does the colleague trust you to complete it?), and the appeal (the task that needs to be completed).

Non-violent Communication

Nonviolent Communication (NVC), created by Marshall Rosenberg, focuses on expressing needs and emotions without judgment, promoting openness and understanding. NVC involves 4 key components:

1. **Observation:** Stating what you observe without interpreting or evaluating. For example, "I notice you didn't respond to my email."

2. **Feelings:** Expressing your emotions related to what you observed. For instance, "I feel worried because the deadline is approaching."

3. **Needs:** Identifying and articulating your unmet needs that are causing these feelings. For example, "I need confirmation that we are on track."

4. **Requests:** Making a clear, actionable request. For instance, "Could you please update me on the project's status?"

NVC encourages empathy and reduces defensiveness, facilitating more genuine and productive conversations. It helps shift the focus from blaming or criticizing to understanding and addressing each other's needs. For example, instead of saying, "You never help with chores," you might say, "I feel overwhelmed with the housework and need more support. Could you help by taking out the trash every evening?"

Reflective Listening

Reflective listening involves actively echoing what others say to confirm understanding and show engagement. It ensures that the speaker feels heard and understood, and it helps clarify any misunderstandings. Here are the key steps:

1. **Paraphrasing:** Restating what the speaker has said in your own words to show that you have understood. For example, "So you're saying that you're feeling stressed about the upcoming presentation?"

2. **Clarifying:** Asking questions to get more information or details. For example, "Can you tell me more about what's causing this stress?"

3. **Summarising:** Recapping the main points of the conversation to ensure you've captured everything accurately. For instance, "To sum up, you're worried about the presentation because of the tight deadline and the importance of the client."

Reflective listening not only shows that you are attentive but also helps to build trust and open lines of communication. It is particularly effective in resolving conflicts and ensuring that all parties feel heard and understood. For example, if a friend shares concerns about their job, you might respond with, "It sounds like you're really stressed about the workload and are worried about meeting your deadlines. Is that right?" This approach helps validate their feelings and opens the door for further discussion.

These tools and techniques provide a structured approach to enhance our communication skills, fostering better relationships and more effective interactions. By integrating these methods into our daily lives, we can improve our ability to understand and be understood, paving the way for clearer and more meaningful connections. Effective communication is not just about talking but about ensuring mutual understanding and cooperation. Whether in personal relationships or professional settings, the ability to communicate effectively is foundational to achieving our collective goals and avoiding the pitfalls of miscommunication.

> "Non-verbal communication is an elaborate secret code that is written nowhere, known by none, and understood by all."
>
> **– Edward Sapir**
>
> "Nothing in life is more important than the ability to communicate effectively."
>
> **– Gerald R. Ford**

Final Thoughts

Effective communication is at the heart of building meaningful relationships, fostering understanding, and making a positive impact on others. Throughout our exploration of communication, we've delved into the nuances of active listening, nonverbal cues, assertive communication, and much more. Each aspect contributes to a comprehensive approach to interacting with others in ways that are constructive, empathetic, and clear. Reflecting on the importance of these skills, it's clear that communication is not merely about exchanging words but about connecting with others on a deeper level. When we actively listen and empathize, we create a space where people feel heard and valued. This deepens our relationships and builds trust, which is essential for both personal and professional growth. As George Bernard Shaw wisely noted, "The single biggest problem in communication is the illusion that it has taken place." True communication goes beyond words; it involves understanding the emotions and intentions behind them.

Moreover, improving our communication skills requires ongoing practice and reflection. Just as with any other skill, we can continually refine our ability to express ourselves and understand others. Techniques like the Four-Sides Model of Communication, Nonviolent Communication, and Reflective Listening provide practical frameworks that we can incorporate into our daily interactions. These methods help us navigate complex conversations, resolve conflicts, and convey our messages more effectively. By committing to continuous improvement in communication, we open ourselves to more profound and meaningful interactions. This commitment involves being aware of our communication habits, seeking feedback, and being willing to adapt. It's about recognizing the impact our words and actions have on others and striving to make that impact as positive as possible.

Effective communication is also crucial in professional settings. It enhances teamwork, drives collaboration, and fosters a positive work environment. When team members communicate clearly and empathetically, they can work together more effectively, address issues proactively, and support each other's growth. This not only improves productivity but also creates a workplace culture where everyone feels respected and valued. In conclusion, mastering the art of communication is essential for personal fulfillment and professional success. It enables us to build strong relationships, foster mutual understanding, and positively influence those around us. As we continue to practice and refine our communication skills, we will find that our interactions become more meaningful, our connections deeper, and our impact greater. Remember, the journey to becoming a better communicator is ongoing, and each step taken brings us closer to achieving more profound and lasting relationships.

> "Don't talk unless you can improve the silence."
>
> **– Jorge Luis Borges**

Communication

1. Listening Log

 - Am I listening or interrupting?
 - Am I improving on this super power

2. Reading
 - Am I reading things
 - Related to my job
 - Related to my department
 - Related to my business
 - Related to my Company
   - Whatever i am passionate about

3. Writing
 - Is my writing of emails ; inter departmental memos; reports improving ?
 - Is my communication with external agencies (Govt; Customer) improving?

NOTES

What did I learn?

`
`
`
`
`

What will I do differently?

`
`
`
`
`

Chapter 4
Behavior

"If you care too much about being praised, in the end you will not accomplish anything serious."

"Let the judgments of others be the consequence of your deeds, not their purpose."

"The best exercise for gaining strength is not missing workouts."

– James Clear

Introduction

"Your beliefs become your thoughts, your thoughts become your words, your words become your actions, your actions become your habits, your habits become your values, and your values become your destiny."

– Mahatma Gandhi

Behavior is an intricate part of who we are, shaped by our beliefs and thoughts, and in turn, shaping our character and relationships. To understand behavior more deeply, it's helpful to divide it into three parts: individual behavior when no one is watching, group behavior, and a combination of both when a task is assigned. At its core, behavior is our response to various situations we encounter daily. Whether it's tackling a task, engaging in competition, pursuing an aspiration, or striving for any life goal, behavior plays a pivotal role in determining our success and fulfillment. One critical aspect of behavior is its inherent blind spot. Often, we are oblivious to the issues our behavior causes because we see it only from our perspective. We fail to recognize its impact on others, including society, friends, and family. This blind spot makes it crucial to develop awareness of our behavior as early as possible.

The primary goal of this chapter is to make us aware of our behavior. Awareness is the first step toward change. Once we are aware, whether we choose to act on that awareness to change our behavior depends on our commitment and circumstances. Sometimes, even when our behavior is obviously flawed, we might continue with it due to our environment or situations. However, one thing is certain: any successful person is keenly aware of their behavior, particularly their shortcomings. It's not always necessary to overhaul our entire behavior. Instead, we can focus on avoiding specific shortcomings whenever possible. This chapter will outline the importance of understanding our behavior and provide tools and techniques to help us become fully aware of our actions and make changes if required.

Developing awareness of our behavior is a lifelong journey. It involves consistently applying techniques to stay mindful of our actions and their impact. By doing so, we set ourselves on the right path toward personal growth and improved interactions with others. As we explore the various facets of behavior, remember that awareness is the foundation. What we choose to do with that awareness is up to us, but being aware is the first, most crucial step.

1. The Behavior-Belief Connection

Our behaviors are intricately linked to our personal beliefs, much like an iceberg. The visible tip of the iceberg represents our actions, while the vast, submerged part symbolizes the underlying beliefs and thoughts that drive those actions. Understanding this connection can help us shape our behaviors more consciously and align them with our values. Imagine your beliefs as the foundation of a building. They provide the stability and structure upon which everything else stands. If the foundation is strong and well-constructed, the building stands tall and firm. Similarly, when our beliefs are positive and constructive, they support behaviors that reflect those qualities. But if the foundation is weak or flawed, the building may collapse or show signs of instability. This analogy underscores the importance of nurturing healthy beliefs to support desirable behaviors.

Consider the belief in honesty. If you hold this belief deeply, it influences your thoughts, encouraging you to value truth and transparency. These thoughts then guide your actions—you speak the truth, admit your mistakes, and build trust with others. Over time, these actions become habitual, forming a part of your character. As Johann Wolfgang von Goethe said, "Behavior is the mirror in which everyone shows their image." Your behavior, shaped by the belief in honesty, mirrors your inner values. The iceberg analogy further illustrates this concept. The submerged part, representing our beliefs, might not be immediately visible, but it profoundly impacts what is seen above the surface—our actions. For instance, someone who believes that helping others is vital will naturally exhibit behaviors of generosity and compassion. Their actions, such as volunteering or assisting a colleague, stem from their core belief in the value of helping others.

It's crucial to recognize that not all beliefs are beneficial. Some may stem from past experiences or cultural conditioning and may not serve us well. For example, if someone holds the belief that they are not good enough, it can lead to self-doubt and behaviors that reflect insecurity. This belief can manifest in avoiding challenges or not speaking up, which can hinder personal and professional growth. To improve our behaviors, we must first examine and adjust our beliefs. This process involves self-reflection and sometimes challenging long-held notions. It's about asking ourselves why we believe what we do and considering if these beliefs help us become the person we want to be. For instance, shifting from a belief of self-doubt to one of self-empowerment can transform our actions from hesitation to assertiveness.

Incorporating empathy into our belief system can also enhance our behaviors. Believing in the importance of understanding and connecting with others on an emotional level fosters behaviors that reflect empathy and compassion. This belief leads us to listen more intently, respond more thoughtfully, and build stronger, more meaningful relationships. Our behaviors are a direct reflection of our beliefs. By understanding and consciously shaping our beliefs, we can influence our actions positively. Just as the iceberg's submerged part holds the bulk of its mass, our beliefs hold the power to shape our visible behaviors. Through self-reflection and a willingness to challenge and adjust our beliefs, we can cultivate behaviors that align with our values and lead to a more fulfilling life.

Take, for example, the belief in fairness. If someone believes deeply in treating everyone equally, this belief will permeate their thoughts and actions. They will make decisions that reflect fairness, such as giving credit where it's due and ensuring everyone has an equal opportunity to contribute. These actions, repeated over time, build a reputation for fairness and integrity, shaping how others perceive them and how they interact with the world. Another crucial aspect is how we treat others, especially those who cannot offer us anything in return. As Abigail Van Buren aptly put it, "The best index to a person's character is how he treats people who can't do him any good, and how he treats people who can't fight back." This belief in the inherent worth of every individual, regardless of their status, shapes behaviors that reflect respect, kindness, and genuine concern for others.

Beliefs also influence our reactions to adversity. Someone who believes in resilience and the ability to overcome obstacles will approach challenges with a problem-solving mindset. They won't see setbacks as failures but as opportunities to learn and grow. This positive belief transforms their actions, making them more likely to persevere and find solutions rather than give up. In the workplace, beliefs about teamwork and collaboration can significantly impact behavior. If a person believes that collaboration leads to better outcomes, they will actively seek input from colleagues, share knowledge, and support team efforts. This belief fosters a collaborative environment, leading to more effective teamwork and better results.

On a personal level, beliefs about health and well-being shape daily habits. Someone who believes in the importance of physical fitness will prioritize exercise and healthy eating. These actions, rooted in their belief about the value of health, become habits that contribute to their overall well-being. In essence, our beliefs are the hidden drivers of our actions. By bringing awareness to these underlying beliefs and making conscious choices to align them with our values, we can create a positive ripple effect in our behaviors. This process of aligning beliefs with actions not only helps us achieve personal growth but also enhances our interactions with others, leading to more harmonious and fulfilling relationships.

By reflecting on and adjusting our beliefs, we can ensure that our actions consistently reflect our true values and aspirations. This alignment between belief and behavior is the cornerstone of authenticity and integrity, guiding us toward a life that is both meaningful and impactful.

Key Takeaways

Our actions are deeply rooted in our personal beliefs, much like the visible tip of an iceberg is supported by its submerged base. Healthy, positive beliefs create a strong foundation for constructive behaviors. Beliefs like honesty, empathy, and fairness guide our thoughts, which in turn shape our actions. For instance, a belief in honesty leads to truthful actions, while empathy fosters compassionate behavior. It's crucial to regularly examine and adjust our beliefs, as not all beliefs are beneficial. By challenging and refining our beliefs, we can ensure that our actions consistently reflect our true values and aspirations. This alignment between belief and behavior is the cornerstone of authenticity and integrity, guiding us toward a life that is both meaningful and impactful.

2. Cultivating Positive Habits

Establishing positive habits is crucial for personal growth and success. Imagine habit formation as creating well-worn paths in a forest. The more you walk along a particular path, the clearer and easier it becomes to follow. Similarly, when you consistently perform positive actions, they become ingrained in your daily routine, making them second nature. Think of habits like brushing your teeth or exercising regularly. These actions, when repeated consistently, become automatic, requiring less conscious effort over time. This is because our brains are wired to develop habits as a way to conserve energy and streamline our daily routines. By focusing on cultivating positive habits, we can harness this natural tendency to improve our lives.

Consistency is key in forming positive habits. It's not about making grand gestures but about small, manageable actions repeated regularly. For example, if you want to develop a habit of reading, start with just 10 minutes a day. Over time, as this becomes a regular part of your routine, you can gradually increase the time. The important thing is to start small and be consistent. Creating positive habits also involves replacing negative ones. This requires self-awareness and a willingness to change. For instance, if you have a habit of checking your phone first thing in the morning, try replacing it with a more positive action like stretching or meditating. By consciously choosing positive actions, you can gradually phase out negative behaviors.

One effective strategy for habit formation is to tie new habits to existing ones. This is known as habit stacking. For example, if you want to start a habit of journaling, do it right after your morning coffee. Linking the new habit to an established one helps to anchor it in your routine, making it more likely to stick. Cultivating positive habits is not only about individual actions but also about creating an environment that supports them. Surround yourself with people who encourage and inspire you, and eliminate distractions that hinder your progress. A supportive environment can significantly enhance your ability to form and maintain positive habits.

Positive habits are powerful because they lead to cumulative benefits over time. Each small, positive action builds on the previous one, creating a compounding effect that significantly impacts your overall well-being. Whether it's improving your health, increasing productivity, or fostering better relationships, the consistent practice of positive habits can lead to substantial, long-term improvements in your life. Moreover, the process of building positive habits often leads to greater self-discipline and resilience. As you continue to reinforce these habits, you develop a stronger sense of control over your actions and decisions. This increased self-efficacy not only helps in maintaining the habits themselves but also empowers you to take on new challenges and pursue larger goals with confidence.

Cultivating positive habits is like carving new paths in a forest. It takes time, effort, and consistency, but once these paths are established, they make your journey smoother and more enjoyable. By focusing on small, manageable actions and creating a supportive environment, you can develop positive habits that lead to lasting personal growth and success.

Key Takeaways

In cultivating positive habits, the key takeaways include understanding the importance of consistency and starting with small, manageable actions. Just as well-worn paths in a forest become easier to navigate over time, regular repetition of positive behaviors embeds them into our routine. It's essential to replace negative habits with positive ones, requiring self-awareness and a commitment to change. Techniques like habit stacking—linking new habits to existing ones—can be highly effective. Additionally, creating a supportive environment and surrounding yourself with encouraging influences can significantly enhance your ability to form and maintain positive habits. By focusing on these strategies, you can develop habits that contribute to lasting personal growth and success.

1. Overcoming Negative Behavior Patterns

Breaking negative behavior patterns is crucial for personal growth. Imagine it like a spider rebuilding its damaged web—deliberate, adaptive, and persistent. To overcome negative behaviors, you first need to identify the triggers. Once you know what sets off these behaviors, practice mindfulness to stay present and aware of your reactions. Another effective strategy is substituting negative behaviors with positive ones. For example, if you tend to snack when stressed, try replacing that habit with a quick walk or deep breathing exercises. It's about understanding what drives these behaviors and actively working to change them. Just like the spider, with patience and the right strategies, you can rebuild your habits to better align with your goals and values.

2. Developing Emotional Intelligence

Developing emotional intelligence is like navigating emotional seas—it helps you manage your behavior in social interactions. Emotional intelligence involves being aware of your own emotions and the emotions of others. This awareness helps guide your interactions, making them more effective and harmonious. Key skills include empathy, self-regulation, and social awareness. By honing these skills, you can improve your relationships, handle conflicts better, and create a more positive social environment. It's about understanding the emotional currents around you and steering your interactions in a way that fosters understanding and connection.

3. Integrity and Values

Think of integrity and core personal values as a compass that directs a traveler. They guide your behavior and decisions, ensuring you stay true to yourself and your principles. Integrity means being honest and having strong moral principles, while values are the fundamental beliefs that shape your actions and attitudes. By aligning your behavior with your values, you build trust and credibility with others. This alignment provides a clear sense of direction, helping you navigate life's challenges with confidence and clarity. When you act with integrity, you not only gain respect from others but also maintain your self-respect and dignity.

4. Self-awareness and Self-regulation

Self-awareness and self-regulation are key to understanding and managing your emotions. Self-awareness involves recognizing your emotions, thoughts, and behaviors. Self-regulation is about controlling your reactions and adapting to different situations. Together, these skills help you respond to challenges in a measured and thoughtful manner. Think of them as a built-in thermostat that helps maintain emotional balance. By developing self-awareness and self-regulation, you can improve your emotional resilience, make better decisions, and build stronger relationships. It's about being in tune with yourself and managing your responses in a way that benefits both you and those around you.

Understanding and practicing these concepts—overcoming negative behaviors, developing emotional intelligence, adhering to integrity and values, and fostering self-awareness and self-regulation—provides a solid foundation for personal development. These skills help you navigate life more effectively, build meaningful relationships, and align your actions with your true self.

Key Tools and Techniques

Understanding behavior involves delving into various psychological concepts and frameworks that can guide our actions and help us cultivate positive habits. In this section, we'll explore three key tools and techniques that provide valuable insights into human behavior: Maslow's Hierarchy of Needs, Operant Conditioning, and the Habit Loop (Cue-Routine-Reward).

Maslow's Hierarchy of Needs: Do Different Levels of Needs Influence Behavior?

Maslow's Hierarchy of Needs is a psychological theory proposed by Abraham Maslow in 1943. It suggests that human behavior is motivated by a series of hierarchical needs, ranging from basic physiological necessities to self-actualization. Imagine this hierarchy as a pyramid with 5 levels. At the base are physiological needs like food, water, and shelter. Once these are met, we seek safety, followed by social needs such as love and belonging. The fourth level is esteem, which includes the need for respect and recognition. At the pinnacle is self-actualization, where we strive to achieve our full potential and pursue personal growth.

Understanding this hierarchy helps us recognize why certain behaviors occur. For example, if someone is struggling to meet their basic needs, their behavior will be focused on survival rather than social interaction or personal growth. By ensuring our foundational needs are met, we can focus on higher-level pursuits, leading to more fulfilling and positive behaviors.

Let's break down the levels for a clearer understanding:

- **Physiological Needs**: These are the basic requirements for human survival, such as air, water, food, shelter, and sleep. When these needs are not met, our focus is entirely on fulfilling them.

- **Safety Needs**: Once physiological needs are satisfied, our attention shifts to safety and security. This includes personal and financial security, health, and well-being. In a modern context, it could be job security or a safe living environment.

- **Love and Belongingness**: At this stage, social relationships become important. We seek friendships, romantic attachments, and family bonds. Humans have an inherent need to belong and be accepted by others.

- **Esteem Needs**: Esteem involves self-respect and the respect of others. This can be achieved through achievements, status, recognition, and respect. It's about feeling valued and confident in our abilities.

- **Self-Actualization**: This is the highest level of Maslow's pyramid. Self-actualization refers to realizing and fulfilling one's potential and seeking personal growth and peak experiences. It's about becoming the most that one can be.

Maslow's theory implies that we are motivated to fulfill these needs in sequence. For example, it's difficult to focus on building meaningful relationships if you're worried about where your next meal is coming from.

Similarly, achieving self-actualization requires that lower-level needs, like esteem and social connections, are already met. This understanding can help us empathize with others and recognize the different stages they might be in their journey.

Operant Conditioning: Can Behavior Be Shaped by Consequences?

Operant Conditioning, developed by B.F. Skinner, is a learning theory that explains how behavior is shaped by its consequences. This concept revolves around the idea that behaviors followed by positive outcomes are likely to be repeated, while those followed by negative outcomes are less likely to recur. It's all about rewards and punishments. In practical terms, this means we can influence behavior by controlling the consequences. For instance, if you want to encourage a child to do their homework, you might offer praise or a small reward when they complete it. Conversely, if they avoid their homework, they might lose certain privileges. Over time, the child learns to associate doing homework with positive reinforcement, increasing the likelihood of this behavior.

Operant Conditioning isn't limited to children; it's a powerful tool in adult life as well. In a work setting, employees are more likely to repeat behaviors that are rewarded, such as meeting deadlines or exceeding performance goals. By understanding and applying these principles, we can shape our own behaviors and those of others to achieve desired outcomes.

Skinner identified different types of reinforcement:

- **Positive Reinforcement**: Adding a rewarding stimulus after a behaviour to increase the likelihood of that behaviour being repeated. For example, giving a compliment for a job well done.

- **Negative Reinforcement**: Removing an aversive stimulus after a behaviour to increase the likelihood of that behaviour being repeated. For example, taking away a tedious task when an employee performs well.

- **Positive Punishment**: Adding an aversive stimulus to decrease a behaviour. For instance, implementing a fine for breaking company rules.

- **Negative Punishment**: Removing a rewarding stimulus to decrease a behaviour. For example, taking away privileges if certain behaviors are exhibited.

These principles can be used in various settings, from parenting and education to workplace management, to encourage desirable behaviors and discourage undesirable ones.

Habit Loop (Cue-Routine-Reward): How Are Habits Formed and How Can They Be Modified for Better Outcomes?

The Habit Loop is a concept popularized by Charles Duhigg in his book, "The Power of Habit." It describes the process through which habits are formed and how they can be changed. The loop consists of 3 components: the cue, the routine, and the reward.

- **Cue:** This is the trigger that initiates the behaviour. It could be a specific time of day, an emotional state, or an environmental factor.

- **Routine:** This is the behaviour itself, the action you take in response to the cue.

- **Reward**: This is the benefit you gain from the behaviour, which reinforces the habit.

For example, imagine you have a habit of eating a cookie every afternoon. The cue might be the time of day (3 PM), the routine is eating the cookie, and the reward is the pleasure you get from the sweet treat. To change this habit, you need to identify the cue and substitute a different routine that offers a similar reward. Instead of a cookie, you might choose to eat a piece of fruit or go for a short walk, which can provide a sense of satisfaction or an energy boost. By understanding the Habit Loop, we can break down our habits and make conscious changes to improve our behaviors. This technique is particularly useful for cultivating positive habits and eliminating negative ones. Whether it's incorporating regular exercise into your routine or reducing screen time, the Habit Loop provides a framework for sustainable behavioral change.

Duhigg emphasizes that understanding these elements allows us to take control of our habits. By recognizing the cues and rewards, we can alter our routines and form healthier habits. For example, if the cue is stress and the routine is smoking a cigarette for relief, recognizing this pattern can help in finding a healthier routine, like deep breathing exercises, that provides the same reward of stress relief.

These tools and techniques offer valuable insights into human behavior, helping us understand why we act the way we do and how we can make positive changes. By applying Maslow's Hierarchy of Needs, Operant Conditioning, and the Habit Loop, we can cultivate behaviors that lead to personal growth, improved relationships, and overall well-being.

Early in my career, I attended a training session on behaviour where I learned a very important lesson. Simply put, it's called 'Verify and Clarify'. Whenever one has doubt regarding communication or conflict or simply when you feel like just asking, use the principle of verifying and clarifying. By using this simple tool, one can verify facts when in doubt or clarify any confusion, etc. I recommend using this simple tool not only in critical junctures but as a way of life whenever you feel like you are in doubt or just need to clear anything that's bothering you. This way all communication gaps can be cleared.

> Theoretical physicist Lisa Randall on looking beyond what we are familiar with:
>
> "In the history of physics, every time we've looked beyond the scales and energies we were familiar with, we've found things that we wouldn't have thought were there. You look inside the atom and eventually you discover quarks. Who would have thought that? It's hubris to think that the way we see things is everything there is."
>
> **– Lisa Randall**

Final Thoughts

As we come to the end of this chapter on behavior, it's crucial to underscore the profound impact our actions have on our lives and the world around us. Mahatma Gandhi once said, "You must be the change you wish to see in the world." This quote encapsulates the essence of intentional behavior. Our behaviors, rooted in our beliefs and values, shape our destinies and influence the lives of those around us. Intentional behavior is about making conscious choices that align with our core values and long-term goals. It involves self-awareness and a commitment to act in ways that reflect our highest ideals. When we live intentionally, our behaviors become a powerful tool for positive change. We start to see that every action, no matter how small, contributes to the broader tapestry of our lives and our communities.

Nelson Mandela's leadership showed us how behavior rooted in forgiveness and reconciliation can transform a nation. Reflecting on our behaviors involves an honest examination of our daily actions and their alignment with our personal values. It's about asking ourselves, "Do my actions reflect who I want to be?" This reflection is not about perfection but about progress. It's a journey of continuous improvement where we strive to align our actions with our values more closely each day.

Cultivating positive habits, as we discussed, is a key aspect of this process. By consistently practicing positive behaviors, we create patterns that reinforce our values and help us achieve our goals. Whether it's through the understanding of Maslow's Hierarchy of Needs, the principles of Operant Conditioning, or the Habit Loop, we have tools at our disposal to shape our behaviors intentionally. Self-awareness and self-regulation are also vital. Understanding our emotional triggers and responses allows us to manage our behaviors more effectively. It helps us respond rather than react, making choices that are thoughtful and aligned with our values. This level of intentionality in behavior not only enhances our personal growth but also positively impacts our relationships and communities.

Moreover, integrity and values act as a compass, guiding us through life's challenges and decisions. Behaving with integrity means staying true to our values even when it's difficult. It's about being honest, reliable, and consistent. These traits build trust and respect, which are foundational to any meaningful relationship. Finally, let's not forget the importance of empathy and emotional intelligence. Understanding and managing our own emotions, and recognizing and influencing the emotions of others, enhances our interactions and builds stronger, more empathetic relationships.

In conclusion, our behaviors are a reflection of our inner beliefs and values. By being intentional about our actions, we craft a life that is not only fulfilling but also impactful. We influence the world positively, one action at a time. As you move forward, I encourage you to reflect on your behaviors and make conscious efforts to align them with your values and goals. This alignment will not only bring personal fulfillment but will also contribute to a better world. Remember, change begins with each one of us, and our actions have the power to shape our destiny and the destiny of those around us.

Sometimes you have to make your own decisions. Nobody will come and save you. Nobody will come and tell you if you're waiting. You will be waiting forever because the decisions that shape your future have to be taken by you. Nobody else, not anyone, not even your parents, not even your siblings, not even your friends, not all your relatives, it's you at the end of the day. It's your decision which counts, it's your decision for which you will be responsible, accountable, and not sometimes but always take your own decision.

– Madhusudan

Jeffrey D. Sachs, an economist and author, on money, spending, and status:

"Living doesn't cost much, but showing off does."

"Unless commitment is made, there are only promises and hopes; but no plans."

– Peter F. Drucker

Behaviour

1. Agree / Disagree

When I, Agree / Disagree

- Am I aware of the impact on deliverables ?
- Am I aware of the conflict ?

2. Ability to say 'No'

Before I say Yes,

- Am I aware as to how much can I chew (capacity)
- Am I aware of what it takes to complete the work (capability and timelines)

4. Verify & Clarify

When in doubt, ask

- Am I dealing with facts or assumptions
- Can I verify facts or seek clarification
- Is my decision based on facts or assumptions

4. Preparation
- Is my behavior based on my preparation (collecting data / analysing data / presenting facts) or am I bluffing

NOTES

What did I learn?

`

`

`

`

`

What will I do differently?

`

`

`

`

`

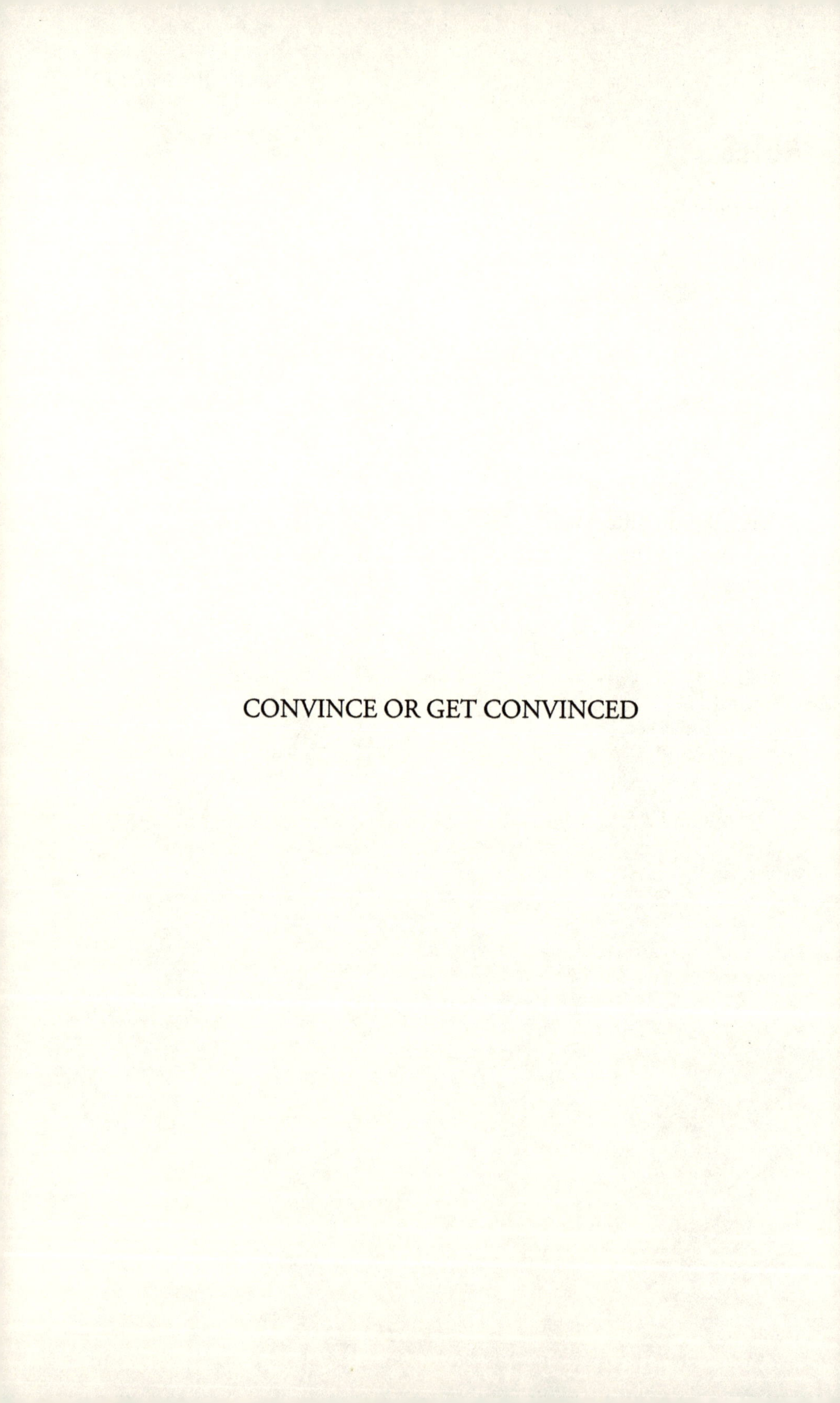

CONVINCE OR GET CONVINCED

Chapter 5
Focus

K(TMT)^2

Keep the main thing the main thing

— Enzo Ferrari

Introduction

"The successful warrior is the average man, with laser-like focus."

— Bruce Lee

In our journey to achieve success, one of the most critical elements is focus. It's not just about being busy or working hard; it's about channeling our energy and efforts into the things that truly matter. Focus has a profound influence on our productivity and goal attainment, shaping the path to our dreams and aspirations. Focus, to me, is about doing one or 2 things in a day and doing them exceptionally well. But before diving deeper, it's important to clarify what focus actually means. Focus is often confused with concentration, but they are distinct concepts. Focus is rooted in our long-term goals, deriving from what we choose to achieve over an extended period. It aligns with the Quadrant 2 activities in the famous 2x2 time management matrix, which emphasizes tasks that are important but not urgent.

To truly understand focus, let's first explore the concepts of attention and concentration. Attention is acute and intense. When we pay attention, we are fully present, like when listening to someone speak. We observe, process, and understand without interruption. Attention is all about being in the moment. Concentration, on the other hand, involves dedicating time to a specific task or activity. It's like reading a book for 30 minutes or practicing a sport for an hour. You immerse yourself in one task before moving on to another. Concentration spreads over multiple tasks but is dedicated to single activities at a time.

Now, focus is broader and more long-term. It's about aspiring to achieve significant goals, such as becoming an athlete, a singer, or an entrepreneur. Focus is tied to aspirations that require sustained effort over time. In essence, attention is acute focus, concentration is medium focus, and focus encompasses all efforts directed toward long-term aspirations. Without clarity on our long-term plans and goals, we cannot fully grasp the essence of focus. It's not about doing things intensely—that's concentration. It's not about doing something outside our plans—that's a distraction. Focus involves choosing one or 2 significant goals to achieve over the next few years and breaking them down into yearly, quarterly, monthly, or weekly plans. It's about consistently taking steps in the right direction.

Many of us fall into the trap of prioritizing immediate tasks that yield short-term results, neglecting to focus on long-term aspirations. Years later, we regret not planning or breaking down our goals into manageable steps. Focus is about reminding ourselves of our long-term plans daily, ensuring we take meaningful actions to progress toward those goals. As Zig Ziglar aptly put it, "Lack of direction, not lack of time, is the problem. We all have twenty-four-hour days." Focus is about maintaining direction and purpose, guiding our efforts to achieve our dreams.

1. Techniques for Improving Concentration and Distraction Management

Improving concentration and managing distractions are essential skills for maintaining focus and achieving long-term goals. Imagine your mind as a muscle that strengthens with the right exercises and techniques. Here are some practical methods to help you enhance your focus and minimize distractions effectively.

First and foremost, let's talk about your environment. Where you work or study can hugely impact how well you can concentrate. A cluttered space often leads to a cluttered mind. Start by keeping your workspace clean and organized. This isn't just about aesthetics; a tidy environment can actually reduce cognitive overload, helping you to focus better. Adjusting your surroundings can also make a big difference. For instance, good lighting can prevent eye strain, and reducing background noise, perhaps with noise-canceling headphones or soft instrumental music, can help maintain your focus. Now, let's move on to cognitive exercises. Your brain, much like any other muscle in your body, benefits from regular workouts. Mindfulness meditation is an excellent way to train your brain to focus. Spending just a few minutes each day meditating can extend your attention span and decrease stress, which in turn makes it easier to concentrate on tasks at hand. Besides meditation, engaging in activities that require sustained mental effort, such as puzzles or reading challenging material, can gradually improve your ability to concentrate over time.

Breaking tasks into smaller, manageable chunks is another effective strategy. This approach is embodied in the Pomodoro Technique, where you work for 25 minutes and then take a 5-minute break. This cycle helps maintain a high level of focus while also preventing burnout. Regular breaks are essential for giving your brain a chance to rest and recharge, leading to better overall productivity. Managing distractions is equally crucial. Start by identifying the most common distractions in your environment and finding ways to minimize them. For example, if your phone is a constant source of distraction, try keeping it on silent mode or out of reach while you work. There are also various apps designed to block access to social media and other distracting websites during work hours.

Creating a to-do list can also help you stay on track and prioritize your tasks. Write down what you need to accomplish each day and stick to the plan. This helps keep you focused on your goals and prevents you from getting sidetracked by less important activities. Additionally, maintaining a healthy lifestyle plays a significant role in enhancing concentration. Regular exercise, a balanced diet, and sufficient sleep are vital for optimal brain function. When your body is well-nourished and rested, your ability to concentrate and manage distractions improves significantly.

Incorporating these techniques into your daily routine can significantly enhance your focus and minimize distractions. Remember, improving concentration is a gradual process that requires consistent effort and practice. By making small adjustments to your environment, practicing mindfulness, breaking tasks into smaller chunks, managing distractions, and maintaining a healthy lifestyle, you can achieve greater focus and productivity. As Ralph Waldo Emerson once said, "Concentration is the secret of strength." With dedicated practice and the right strategies, you can harness the power of concentration to reach your long-term goals.

Key Takeaways

Enhancing concentration and managing distractions involves creating an environment conducive to focus, such as a clutter-free workspace and minimizing digital interruptions. Techniques like setting specific times for deep work and taking regular breaks can help maintain high levels of concentration. Mindfulness practices like meditation and mindful breathing can significantly improve focus by training the mind to stay present. Embracing single-tasking over multitasking enhances efficiency and the quality of work. Lastly, developing a habit of reflecting on daily tasks can help identify and eliminate sources of distraction, leading to better overall productivity.

2. Mindfulness Practices and Single-tasking:

Mindfulness practices and single-tasking are essential tools for enhancing focus and productivity. Let's explore these concepts in detail and understand how they can be effectively implemented to bring significant benefits to our daily lives.

Mindfulness Practices

Mindfulness is about being fully present and engaged in the moment. It involves paying close attention to our thoughts, feelings, and surroundings without judgment. One of the most effective ways to cultivate mindfulness is through meditation. This practice helps train the mind to maintain focus and reduce the mental clutter that often distracts us. A simple meditation practice involves sitting quietly and focusing on your breath. As you breathe in and out, you pay attention to the sensation of the breath entering and leaving your body. Each time your mind wanders—which it inevitably will—you gently bring your attention back to your breath. This exercise strengthens your ability to concentrate over time, making it easier to maintain focus during other activities.

Mindful breathing is another technique that can significantly improve focus. It involves taking slow, deep breaths and concentrating on the physical sensations of breathing. This practice can be done anywhere, anytime, and is particularly useful in moments of stress or distraction. By focusing on your breath, you anchor your mind to the present moment, which helps clear mental distractions and enhance concentration. In addition to meditation and mindful breathing, incorporating mindfulness into everyday activities can also be beneficial. This can include mindful eating, where you pay attention to the taste, texture, and aroma of your food, or mindful walking, where you focus on the sensation of your feet touching the ground and the sights and sounds around you. These practices help to develop a habit of mindfulness that can be carried into other areas of your life, improving overall focus and mental clarity.

Single-tasking

Single-tasking, or focusing on one task at a time, is a practical application of mindfulness. In today's fast-paced world, multitasking is often seen as a necessity. However, research has shown that multitasking can reduce productivity and increase errors. Our brains are not wired to handle multiple tasks simultaneously; instead, they switch rapidly between tasks, which can lead to mental fatigue and decreased efficiency. By contrast, single-tasking allows you to give your full attention to one task at a time, resulting in higher quality work and greater efficiency. When you single-task, you're more likely to enter a state of flow, where you're fully immersed and engaged in the activity. This state not only improves the quality of your work but also makes the task more enjoyable and fulfilling.

To practice single-tasking, start by eliminating distractions. Turn off notifications on your phone and computer, and create a dedicated workspace where you can focus. Set specific times for checking emails and messages so that they don't interrupt your work. Use tools like to-do lists to prioritize tasks and tackle them one by one. Break your work into manageable chunks and take short breaks between tasks to rest and recharge. Another effective strategy for single-tasking is to use the Pomodoro Technique. This involves working on a task for a set period, usually 25 minutes, followed by a short break. This method helps to maintain focus and prevent burnout by balancing periods of intense concentration with regular intervals of rest.

Additionally, it's important to recognize the value of downtime. Taking time to relax and recharge is crucial for maintaining high levels of focus and productivity. Activities such as going for a walk, listening to music, or spending time with loved ones can help clear your mind and reduce stress, making it easier to concentrate when you return to work. In essence, mindfulness practices like meditation and mindful breathing help train the mind to maintain focus, while single-tasking allows for higher quality work by giving full attention to one task at a time. These techniques are essential for anyone looking to improve their concentration and achieve their long-term goals.

By incorporating mindfulness and single-tasking into your daily routine, you can enhance your focus and productivity significantly. These practices help you to be more present, reduce stress, and achieve better results in your work and personal life. Through consistent practice, you'll find that your ability to concentrate improves, leading to greater success and fulfillment in all areas of your life.

Key Takeaways

Mindfulness and single-tasking significantly enhance focus and productivity. Mindfulness involves being fully present, cultivated through practices like meditation and mindful breathing. Single-tasking, or focusing on one task at a time, boosts efficiency and work quality. Strategies like eliminating distractions, setting specific times for emails, and using techniques like Pomodoro are effective. Incorporating these practices into your routine helps achieve long-term goals by improving concentration and reducing stress.

Setting Clear Intentions

Setting clear intentions is crucial for maintaining focus and direction in both personal and professional pursuits. When you have well-defined goals, you create a roadmap that guides your actions and decisions. Clear intentions help to align your daily tasks with your long-term objectives, ensuring that your efforts are purposeful and directed toward achieving meaningful outcomes. Without clear goals, it's easy to get sidetracked and lose focus, leading to wasted time and effort. By setting specific, measurable, achievable, relevant, and time-bound (SMART) goals, you provide yourself with a clear target to aim for, making it easier to stay motivated and on track.

Overcoming Procrastination

Procrastination can be a major obstacle to achieving your goals, but there are strategies to overcome it. One effective approach is to break down large tasks into smaller, more manageable milestones. This makes the task feel less overwhelming and provides a sense of accomplishment as you complete each step. Additionally, it's important to understand the underlying causes of procrastination, such as fear of failure or lack of interest. By addressing these root causes, you can develop more effective strategies to combat procrastination. Techniques like setting deadlines, using a timer (e.g. the Pomodoro Technique), and eliminating distractions can also help to keep you focused and productive.

Deep Work and Flow State

Deep work refers to engaging in complex tasks that require intense focus and cognitive effort. It involves uninterrupted, distraction-free periods of work that allow you to produce high-quality results. Entering a flow state, where you are fully immersed and performing at your peak, often occurs during deep work. In this state, you lose track of time and are completely absorbed in the task at hand, leading to increased productivity and creativity. To achieve deep work and flow, it's essential to minimize distractions, set aside dedicated time for focused work, and tackle challenging tasks that push your skills and abilities. This practice not only enhances your productivity but also leads to greater satisfaction and fulfillment in your work.

Key Tools and Techniques

Deep Work

Deep work is all about setting aside uninterrupted time to tackle challenging tasks that require your full concentration. This concept, introduced by Cal Newport, emphasizes creating an environment where distractions are minimized so you can focus intensely and produce high-quality work efficiently. Think of deep work as diving into a pool of concentration. You want to eliminate anything that might pull you back to the surface. This could mean scheduling specific blocks of time in your day when you won't be disturbed, turning off phone notifications, and finding a quiet space to work. The idea is to get into a state where your mind is fully engaged with the task at hand.

Here are some practical steps to help you get into deep work:

1. **Time Blocking**: Set specific times for deep work and stick to them. This routine trains your brain to be ready to focus during these periods.

2. **Eliminating Distractions**: Shut off notifications, close unrelated browser tabs, and let people know you're in deep work mode to avoid interruptions.

3. **Setting Clear Goals**: Know what you want to achieve during your deep work session. Clear objectives keep you focused and help you measure your progress.

4. **Taking Breaks**: Deep work can be tiring, so it's important to take regular breaks to recharge. Try the Pomodoro Technique—25 minutes of focused work followed by a 5-minute break.

By practicing deep work regularly, you'll improve your ability to handle complex tasks, boost your productivity, and achieve more in both your personal and professional life.

Flow State

Achieving a flow state is like getting lost in the zone where everything clicks, and you're fully immersed in what you're doing. This concept, described by psychologist Mihaly Csikszentmihalyi, is about being completely absorbed in an activity, losing track of time, and enjoying the process. The key to entering a flow state is finding a balance between the challenge of the task and your skill level. If the task is too easy, you'll get bored; if it's too hard, you'll get frustrated. The sweet spot is where the task pushes your abilities just enough to keep you engaged and motivated.

To reach a flow state, consider these tips:

1. **Set Clear Goals**: Just like with deep work, having clear objectives helps you stay focused and gives you a sense of direction.

2. **Match Skills to Challenges**: Choose tasks that are challenging but doable. This keeps you engaged and helps you stretch your abilities.

3. **Eliminate Distractions**: Create a distraction-free environment to maintain the intense focus needed for a flow state. Ensure your workspace supports uninterrupted work.

4. **Immediate Feedback**: Seek out or create opportunities for immediate feedback. This helps you stay on track and adjust your efforts in real time, enhancing your engagement and performance.

5. **Intrinsic Motivation**: Engage in activities that you find inherently rewarding and enjoyable. Passion for the task at hand is a significant driver for entering the flow state.

Experiencing flow can lead to higher productivity, creativity, and satisfaction. It transforms challenging tasks into enjoyable activities, making it easier to achieve peak performance and derive joy from your work.

By incorporating deep work and striving to achieve flow states, you can maximize your focus, enhance your productivity, and find greater fulfillment in your personal and professional pursuits.

The Pomodoro Technique

The Pomodoro Technique is a popular time management method designed to improve focus and productivity. Developed by Francesco Cirillo in the late 1980s, this technique uses a timer to break work into intervals, traditionally 25 minutes in length, separated by short breaks. Each interval is known as a "Pomodoro," named after the tomato-shaped kitchen timer that Cirillo used as a university student.

Here's how the Pomodoro Technique works:

1. **Choose a Task**: Start by selecting a task you want to work on. It could be anything from writing an article to studying for an exam or working on a project.

2. **Set the Timer**: Set a timer for 25 minutes. During this period, focus entirely on the task at hand, avoiding any distractions. This period of intense focus is designed to make the most of your concentration.

3. **Work on the Task**: Work continuously until the timer goes off. The key is to work with full concentration and avoid interruptions during these 25 minutes.

4. **Take a Short Break**: Once the timer rings, take a 5-minute break. Use this time to relax, stretch, or grab a quick snack. This break helps to refresh your mind and maintain your productivity throughout the day.

5. **Repeat the Process**: After four Pomodoros, take a longer break of 15-30 minutes. This extended break helps you recharge before starting the cycle again.

The Pomodoro Technique is effective because it encourages sustained focus and regular breaks, preventing burnout and maintaining high levels of productivity. By breaking work into manageable intervals, it makes large tasks feel less overwhelming and promotes a structured approach to work. Incorporating the Pomodoro Technique into your routine can help you manage your time more effectively, stay focused, and achieve your goals with greater efficiency.

> "Many times in life, the decision is not whether to do one thing or another, but when to emphasize one aspect over another.
>
> Rest or train? Research or write? Diversify or concentrate?
>
> Opposite answers can both be right. The question is: which one is the right answer for right now."
>
> **– James Clear**

Conclusion

As we wrap up our exploration of focus, it's essential to recognize that focus is not just a skill; it's a fundamental aspect of living a successful and fulfilling life. The ability to concentrate on what truly matters can transform challenges into achievements, turning aspirations into reality. It's the driving force behind progress, enabling us to navigate the complexities of our daily lives with clarity and purpose. Practicing the techniques we've discussed—like mindfulness, setting clear intentions, and utilizing methods such as the Pomodoro Technique—can sharpen your focus and enhance your effectiveness in various aspects of life. These strategies are not just about improving productivity; they're about fostering a deeper connection to your goals and values, ensuring that your actions align with your long-term aspirations.

Remember, focus is about making conscious choices and committing to them. It's about prioritizing what truly matters, despite the distractions and noise of everyday life. By cultivating this skill, you can create a more directed and meaningful path, one that leads to personal growth and success. So, as you go forward, I encourage you to practice these techniques, be patient with yourself, and stay committed to your goals. With sustained effort and a clear focus, you can achieve remarkable things and lead a life filled with purpose and achievement.

A few definitions and quotes that I found interesting, and I think understanding these will further clarify what focus is all about. Also, it helps clarify what attention and concentration are about.

> "Focus is the art of knowing what to ignore."
>
> **– James Clear**
>
> "In a museum, you need to spend at least 10 minutes with an artwork to truly see it. Aim to view 5 pieces at 10 minutes each rather than 100 at 30 seconds each."
>
> **– Kevin Kelly**
>
> "When you are stuck or overwhelmed, focus on the smallest possible thing that moves your project forward."
>
> **– Kevin Kelly**

- Attention is the ability to actively process specific information in the environment while tuning out other details. Attention is limited in terms of both capacity and duration, so it is important to have ways to effectively manage the attentional resources we have available in order to make sense of the world.

- "Attention is being keenly alive to some specific factors in our environment. It is a preparatory adjustment for response." - Morgan. Thus, attention is essentially a process and not a product.

- The attention definition in psychology is a cognitive process that involves observing or becoming aware of something. Some examples of types of attention in psychology are focused, selective, sustained, divided, and alternating attention.

Dumvillev: Attention is the concentration of consciousness on one object rather than on another.

Thus, according to Kahneman's theory, every instance of attention is an instance of effort, and every instance of effort is an instance of attention. This identification of effort and attention appears to resolve Q2 – effort is a special case of cognitive activity; it is attention.

Attention is always changing. (ii) Attention is always an active center of our experience. (iii) It is selective. (iv) Attention is continuous.

Concentration

The ability to give all your attention or effort to something

Concentration - concentratio, action or an act of coming together at a single place, bringing to a common center, was used in post-classical Latin in 1550 or earlier, similar terms attested in Italian (1589), Spanish (1589), English (1606), French (1632).

Focus: to give all your attention to something

Focus

(Long term oriented)

What are the areas where I need to do build my Capacity & Capability

Area	Action (include timeline)

Do one or two things in a day and do it well - Madhusudan

NOTES

What did I learn?

`

`

`

`

What will I do differently?

`

`

`

`

DO ONE THING IN A DAY AND DO IT WELL

Chapter 6
Growth Mindset

My ambition is handicapped by laziness.

– Charles Bukowski

Introduction

"The only limit to our realization of tomorrow will be our doubts of today."

– Franklin D. Roosevelt

In our journey through life, the concept of a growth mindset plays a pivotal role in shaping our personal development and our ability to overcome challenges. A growth mindset is the belief that our abilities and intelligence can be developed through dedication, hard work, and perseverance. This mindset contrasts sharply with a fixed mindset, where individuals believe that their talents and abilities are static and unchangeable. Embracing a growth mindset is essential for achieving success, as it fosters resilience, encourages learning from failure, and fuels continuous improvement.

Understanding and adopting a growth mindset is crucial not just for professional success but also for personal fulfillment. It involves viewing challenges as opportunities to learn, seeing effort as a path to mastery, and understanding that setbacks are not a reflection of one's abilities but a natural part of the growth process. By cultivating a growth mindset, we can break free from the constraints of self-doubt and embrace the limitless possibilities that lie ahead. This chapter will delve into the principles of a growth mindset, provide practical strategies for developing it, and highlight inspiring stories of individuals who have thrived by adopting this powerful perspective.

1. Embracing Challenges and Overcoming Obstacles

Challenges are not roadblocks but stepping stones toward personal growth. Imagine a rock climber facing a tough ascent. Each grip and foothold presents a challenge, but with each one conquered, the climber gains strength, skill, and confidence. Similarly, in life, the obstacles we encounter can be seen as opportunities for development. When we embrace challenges, we push our boundaries and discover new capabilities within ourselves. Viewing difficulties as catalysts for growth transforms our approach to life's hurdles. Instead of seeing a problem as a dead end, we can view it as a chance to learn and improve. This mindset shift is essential for personal and professional development. Embracing challenges helps us build resilience, enhances our problem-solving skills, and fosters a sense of accomplishment. By overcoming obstacles, we not only achieve our goals but also cultivate a stronger, more adaptive mindset that prepares us for future challenges.

Consider Thomas Edison, who famously remarked that he had not failed but found 10,000 ways that didn't work before inventing the light bulb. His perspective on failure and challenges highlights the essence of a growth mindset. Every setback was a learning opportunity, bringing him one step closer to success. This attitude can be applied to our own lives. When we view our challenges as opportunities to learn and grow, we start to see every obstacle as a potential stepping stone to greater achievement. Moreover, embracing challenges requires us to step out of our comfort zones. This might mean taking on new responsibilities at work, learning a new skill, or facing a personal fear. Each of these experiences, though daunting at first, contributes to our growth. By continually pushing ourselves, we become more adaptable and better equipped to handle future challenges.

In essence, developing a growth mindset involves shifting our perception of challenges. Rather than viewing them as insurmountable barriers, we see them as opportunities for learning and growth. This change in perspective can have a profound impact on our personal and professional lives, leading to greater resilience, creativity, and success. Embracing challenges wholeheartedly is a crucial step toward unlocking our full potential and achieving long-term aspirations.

Key Takeaways

Embracing challenges and overcoming obstacles are essential elements of a growth mindset. By viewing challenges as opportunities for growth, we transform our approach to difficulties, seeing them as stepping stones rather than roadblocks. This perspective fosters resilience, enhances problem-solving skills, and builds confidence. The rock climber analogy illustrates how overcoming each obstacle strengthens us, just as Thomas Edison's view on failure highlights the importance of persistence and learning from setbacks. Embracing challenges requires us to step out of our comfort zones, continually pushing our boundaries and preparing us for future hurdles. This mindset shift is crucial for personal and professional development, helping us achieve our goals and unlock our full potential.

2. Learning from Failures

One of the most crucial aspects of a growth mindset is the ability to view failures as opportunities for learning rather than as definitive setbacks. This shift in perspective is essential for fostering resilience and paving the way for success. When we encounter failure, we often feel discouraged, but it's important to recognize that each failure is a stepping stone to greater achievement. Failures provide valuable lessons that can guide our future actions. When Thomas Edison was working on the invention of the light bulb, he famously said, "I have not failed. I've just found 10,000 ways that won't work." This mindset highlights the importance of persistence and the willingness to learn from each unsuccessful attempt. Every failure offers insights that help us refine our strategies and approaches.

Viewing failures as lessons requires a few key practices. First, it involves self-compassion, allowing ourselves to make mistakes without harsh self-criticism. This gentle approach helps maintain motivation and prevents us from becoming discouraged. Second, it necessitates active reflection. By analyzing what went wrong, we can identify areas for improvement and adjust our methods accordingly. This critical assessment is crucial for continuous growth and development. Additionally, overcoming the fear of failure is vital. Often, fear of failing can paralyze us, preventing us from taking necessary risks. Embracing failure as a natural part of the learning process liberates us from this fear and encourages us to take bold steps toward our goals. Recognizing that failure is not the end but rather a part of the journey helps us remain resilient and persistent.

Moreover, sharing our failures and the lessons learned can be incredibly powerful. By openly discussing our mistakes, we normalize the experience of failure and create an environment where others feel safe to take risks and innovate. This culture of transparency and learning fosters collective growth and encourages everyone to learn from each other's experiences. Failure also helps build character. It teaches humility, patience, and perseverance. When we fail and rise again, we develop a stronger sense of self and a deeper understanding of our capabilities. This resilience not only aids in achieving our goals but also equips us to handle future challenges with greater confidence and composure.

Ultimately, adopting a growth mindset toward failure involves viewing each setback as a chance to grow and improve. It's about understanding that failure is not a reflection of our worth but a part of the process of becoming better and more capable. By embracing failure with a positive and proactive attitude, we can turn obstacles into opportunities and setbacks into stepping stones toward success.

Key Takeaways

We should understand that failures are valuable lessons rather than setbacks. Embracing this perspective fosters resilience, allowing us to view challenges as opportunities for growth. Reflecting on failures helps us refine our strategies and avoid repeating mistakes. Overcoming the fear of failure encourages us to take necessary risks, promoting innovation and progress. Sharing our failures can create a supportive environment where others feel safe to learn and grow. Ultimately, a positive attitude toward failure builds character and equips us to handle future challenges with confidence.

3. Resilience and Perseverance

Resilience and perseverance are essential components of a growth mindset. Building resilience involves adopting strategies that enable us to maintain a positive attitude and view setbacks as opportunities for growth. One effective approach is reframing our perspective on failure. Instead of seeing it as a defeat, we can consider it a valuable lesson. For example, if a project at work doesn't go as planned, instead of dwelling on the failure, we can analyze what went wrong, understand the factors that led to the outcome, and use this insight to improve future efforts. This process not only builds resilience but also encourages a proactive approach to problem-solving.

A key aspect of resilience is maintaining a positive attitude. This means focusing on what we can control and finding ways to stay optimistic, even in difficult circumstances. Positive self-talk, mindfulness practices, and maintaining a supportive network of friends and family can help bolster our resilience. It's also important to set realistic goals and break larger challenges into smaller, manageable tasks. Celebrating small victories along the way can provide motivation and reinforce our belief in our ability to overcome obstacles. Another important element is balancing effort and talent. While innate talent can provide an initial advantage, it is often persistent effort that leads to long-term success. This is evident in many stories of individuals who, despite not being the most naturally gifted, achieved remarkable success through sheer determination and hard work. Emphasizing the importance of consistent effort helps us understand that perseverance can often surpass natural talent. When we commit to putting in the effort, refining our skills, and learning from our experiences, we set ourselves on a path to continuous improvement and eventual success.

Developing resilience also involves being adaptable and open to change. Life is unpredictable, and being able to adjust our plans and strategies in response to new challenges is crucial. This adaptability allows us to stay focused on our goals while navigating the uncertainties that come our way. Building a strong support system is equally important. Surrounding ourselves with people who provide encouragement, constructive feedback, and perspective can make a significant difference in our ability to persevere through tough times. Self-compassion is another crucial factor. Being kind to ourselves, especially when we encounter setbacks, helps us maintain our mental and emotional well-being. Recognizing that everyone faces challenges and that setbacks are a natural part of the growth process can reduce self-criticism and increase our resilience.

In practical terms, developing resilience and perseverance involves setting clear goals, creating action plans, and regularly assessing our progress. It means being willing to put in the effort required to achieve our goals and staying committed even when the going gets tough. By focusing on effort and learning rather than just outcomes, we cultivate the resilience needed to persevere through any challenge, ultimately leading to personal and professional growth.

Key Takeaways

Developing resilience and perseverance is crucial for achieving long-term success. Recognize that setbacks and failures are opportunities for growth and learning. Maintain a positive attitude by focusing on what you can control and celebrating small victories along the way. Balance effort and talent by committing to persistent effort and hard work, understanding that perseverance often surpasses innate ability. Adaptability and self-compassion are key, allowing you to adjust your plans and be kind to yourself during challenges. Building a supportive network of friends and family can provide the encouragement needed to persevere through tough times.

Continuous Improvement and Lifelong Learning

Adopting a mindset of continuous improvement means treating every experience as an opportunity to learn. This keeps us open to new knowledge and ready to expand our horizons. Self-regulation and deliberate practice are key here; setting goals, monitoring progress, and refining skills through focused efforts help us grow personally and professionally.

Positive Self-talk and Emotional Management

Positive self-talk is crucial for maintaining motivation and overcoming challenges. By replacing negative thoughts with affirmations, we boost our resilience. Emotional intelligence, which involves understanding and managing our emotions, helps us respond constructively to challenges, fostering a growth-oriented mindset.

By embracing a growth mindset, we commit to continuous improvement, seeing each challenge as an opportunity to learn and grow. The transformation isn't always easy, but it's through these trials that we develop the strength, skills, and perspectives necessary to achieve our fullest potential. When we finally emerge, the rewards of our perseverance are evident in our newfound capabilities and the expanded horizons before us. The journey of the caterpillar to a butterfly teaches us that personal change and development are possible for anyone willing to embrace a growth mindset. It reminds us that, no matter where we start, we have the power to transform our lives through dedication and perseverance.

Key Tools and Techniques

Developing a growth mindset involves using specific tools and techniques that help navigate the journey of continuous improvement and overcoming obstacles. Here are some key methods to consider:

The Dip

Experiencing dips and challenges is a normal part of the growth process. Seth Godin, in his book "The Dip," elaborates on this concept, explaining how almost every significant endeavor encounters a period of stagnation or difficulty—a dip—where progress slows, and the outcome becomes uncertain. This phase is often the most testing and can severely challenge our commitment and resilience. Understanding that dips are natural and expected in any significant endeavor helps us mentally prepare for these challenges. Instead of viewing them as insurmountable obstacles, we should see dips as necessary hurdles that filter out those who lack the perseverance to push through. This mindset shift is crucial because it changes our perception of difficulties from being barriers to being integral parts of the journey toward success.

Imagine you're working on a long-term project. At the start, you're filled with enthusiasm and ideas. However, as time progresses, you might hit a point where progress seems slow, motivation wanes, and the initial excitement fades. This is the dip. It's at this point that many people give up, thinking they are not cut out for the task or that the goal is unattainable. However, those who understand the concept of the dip recognize that this is a critical moment. They know that pushing through the dip is where real growth and learning happen. Godin emphasizes that not all dips are worth pushing through. Some endeavors are dead ends, and part of the wisdom lies in recognizing which dips are worth the effort. The key is to discern whether the challenge you're facing is a dip—a temporary setback that, once overcome, will lead to greater rewards—or a cul-de-sac, where no amount of effort will yield success.

For instance, consider a student struggling with a challenging subject. Initially, they might find the material difficult and feel discouraged. However, with persistence, seeking help, and dedicating more time to study, they can overcome the dip and achieve mastery. The same applies to entrepreneurs who face market downturns or athletes who experience performance plateaus. Recognizing the dip, embracing it, and pushing through can lead to significant breakthroughs and long-term success. The idea of the dip teaches us that persistence is often what separates those who succeed from those who give up. By expecting and preparing for these challenging periods, we can better navigate them and come out stronger on the other side. It's this persistence, the ability to keep going when things get tough, that truly defines a growth mindset and leads to achieving our most significant goals.

Deliberate Practice

Deliberate practice is a concept popularized by psychologist Anders Ericsson, which differentiates from mere repetition or general practice by its structured, purposeful, and feedback-oriented nature. Unlike routine practice, where one might perform tasks repeatedly without specific goals, deliberate practice involves highly focused efforts to improve specific aspects of a skill. This method is particularly effective for mastering complex tasks and achieving high levels of expertise.

The Components of Deliberate Practice

1. **Specific Goals**: Deliberate practice begins with clearly defined objectives. Instead of vague aims like "get better at piano," the goals are precise, such as "improve my left-hand coordination in a specific piece." This precision allows for targeted efforts and measurable progress.

2. **Focused Effort**: This practice requires intense concentration and effort. It's not about mindlessly going through the motions but actively engaging with the task at hand. Each practice session should be mentally taxing, pushing one's abilities beyond their current limits.

3. **Immediate Feedback**: Critical to deliberate practice is receiving and integrating feedback. This can come from teachers, coaches,

peers, or self-assessment. Feedback highlights areas of improvement and helps refine techniques, ensuring that practice is effective rather than reinforcing bad habits.

4. **Repetition with Variation**: While repetition is key, it's not about doing the same thing over and over without variation. Deliberate practice involves repeating tasks but also varying them to address different aspects of the skill. This might mean practicing a piece of music at different tempos or from different sections.

5. **Continuous Refinement**: Deliberate practice is iterative. Practitioners continually refine their skills, setting new challenges as they meet their goals. It's a process of constant improvement and adjustment based on performance and feedback.

Practical Applications

- **Music**: For musicians, deliberate practice might involve breaking down a piece into difficult segments, practicing them slowly, and gradually increasing the tempo as proficiency improves. A violinist might focus on bowing techniques in one session and finger positioning in another, always with specific goals in mind.

- **Sports**: Athletes use deliberate practice by focusing on particular aspects of their performance. A basketball player might spend a session perfecting free throws, analyzing each shot, and adjusting their technique based on feedback from a coach or video review.

- **Academics**: In academic settings, deliberate practice can be applied by targeting weak areas in a subject. A student struggling with maths might work through specific types of problems, seek feedback from a tutor, and use that feedback to adjust their approach.

Benefits of Deliberate Practice

The benefits of deliberate practice are profound. It accelerates learning by focusing efforts on areas that need improvement, making practice time more efficient and effective. It also builds resilience and perseverance, as practitioners learn to handle challenges and setbacks constructively. Moreover, deliberate practice fosters a growth mindset. By continuously striving to improve and embracing the feedback process, individuals develop a belief in their capacity to grow and succeed through effort and learning.

Incorporating deliberate practice into one's routine requires discipline and dedication. It's about making the most of practice time by being strategic, focused, and persistent. This approach to practice not only enhances skill acquisition but also instills a deeper understanding and mastery of the task at hand.

Feedback Loop

The feedback loop is a critical component of learning and growth, emphasizing the continuous cycle of receiving feedback, making adjustments, and improving performance. This concept is vital in various fields, including education, sports, business, and personal development, as it helps individuals and teams refine their skills and strategies through iterative processes.

Components of a Feedback Loop

1. **Observation and Data Collection**: The first step in a feedback loop is to observe and collect data on performance. This can involve self-assessment, peer review, or input from mentors and coaches. The goal is to gather information about what is working well and what needs improvement.

2. **Feedback Delivery**: The collected data is then communicated back to the individual or team. Effective feedback is specific,

constructive, and actionable. Instead of vague comments like "good job" or "needs improvement," detailed insights are provided, such as "your presentation was clear, but you need to work on your pacing and eye contact."

3. **Reflection and Analysis**: After receiving feedback, it's crucial to reflect on the information and analyze it critically. This involves understanding the feedback, recognizing patterns, and identifying areas that require change. Reflection helps in internalizing the feedback and preparing for the next steps.

4. **Action and Adjustment**: The final step is to take action based on the feedback. This could mean altering techniques, adopting new strategies, or focusing on specific skills that need enhancement. The adjustments are then put into practice, leading to improved performance.

5. **Iteration**: The process doesn't end with one cycle. The feedback loop is iterative, meaning it repeats continuously. After making adjustments, performance is observed again, new feedback is gathered, and further improvements are made. This ongoing cycle fosters continuous growth and development.

Practical Applications

- **Education**: In academic settings, teachers use feedback loops to help students improve their learning. Regular assessments, constructive feedback, and opportunities for revision enable students to understand their mistakes and learn from them. For instance, a student may receive feedback on an essay, revise it based on the comments, and then submit a better version.

- **Workplace**: In the professional world, feedback loops are essential for employee development. Managers provide regular performance reviews; employees reflect on the feedback, make necessary adjustments, and improve their work. This continuous process helps in skill development and career advancement.

- **Sports**: Athletes rely on feedback loops to enhance their performance. Coaches observe their performance, provide detailed feedback, and suggest adjustments. Athletes then work on these areas, improving their skills and strategies over time. This process is crucial for achieving peak performance.

- **Personal Development**: Individuals use feedback loops in their personal growth journeys. By seeking feedback from friends, mentors, or through self-assessment, they can identify areas for improvement, make changes, and track their progress over time.

Benefits of a Feedback Loop

The feedback loop offers numerous benefits, including:

1. **Continuous Improvement**: By constantly receiving and acting on feedback, individuals and teams can make incremental improvements, leading to significant progress over time.

2. **Enhanced Performance**: Regular feedback helps in identifying weaknesses and strengths, allowing for targeted improvements that enhance overall performance.

3. **Increased Self-Awareness**: Feedback loops promote self-reflection, helping individuals become more aware of their behaviours, skills, and areas needing improvement.

4. **Motivation and Engagement**: Constructive feedback can motivate individuals by providing clear goals and recognition of their efforts, keeping them engaged and committed to their development.

5. **Better Decision Making**: By using feedback to inform their actions, individuals can make better decisions, avoid repeating mistakes, and adopt more effective strategies.

Incorporating feedback loops into daily practice is a powerful way to achieve continuous growth and success. Whether in personal endeavors, academic pursuits, or professional careers, the cycle of feedback, reflection, and adjustment is a cornerstone of effective development.

Final Thoughts

Adopting a growth mindset is nothing short of transformative. It turns latent potential into actual achievement by fostering resilience, adaptability, and a relentless pursuit of improvement. When we believe that our abilities can be developed through dedication and hard work, we open ourselves up to endless possibilities for growth and success. By cultivating a growth mindset, we equip ourselves to better navigate life's inevitable challenges. Instead of being deterred by obstacles, we learn to view them as opportunities for growth and learning. This shift in perspective not only enhances our personal and professional lives but also empowers us to seize opportunities that come our way.

Embrace the journey of continuous learning and improvement. Each step forward, no matter how small, brings you closer to your goals. Remember, the path to success is not a straight line but a series of adjustments and refinements. Stay committed to your growth, and you'll find that even the most daunting challenges can be overcome with persistence and a positive outlook. As you move forward, keep these principles in mind and make a conscious effort to apply them in your daily life. With a growth mindset, you are not just preparing for success; you are creating it, one step at a time.

One of the ways to improve growth mindset is to read autobiographies of entreprenuers ; founder of the organizations / insttitutions and get inspired by their stories. However, as Naval said, Inspiration is Perishable and hence the learnings must be converted actions as soon as possible.

Read autobiographies widely, listen to podcasts to develop the mindset which propels you towards growth mindset

"A mindset that can take you far in life:

What I want doesn't exist, so I'll create it."

– James Clear

Growth Mindset

1. Did I list down my vision / goals for next 5y
- what kind of growth am I imagining
- Am I building my capacity and capability in that direction

Actions required

Capacity	Capabilities

2. Am I aware of Company's vision and growth plans
- how can I be part of that growth
- What capacities and capabilities that I should build to grow along with the Company

3. Am I generally aware of how the market* is growing (*market related to the business that you are in)

NOTES

What did I learn?

-

-

-

-

What will I do differently?

-

-

-

-

-

Chapter 7
Going Beyond

"Do one thing every day that scares you."

– Eleanor Roosevelt.

Introduction

Life is a vast horizon, and within its expanse lies the potential for endless exploration and adventure. Going beyond isn't just about pushing physical limits; it's a mindset that propels us to transcend our current boundaries, whether they are mental, emotional, or situational. This chapter delves into the spirit of going beyond, urging us to embrace the unknown and stretch our capabilities. Before we understand what going beyond entails, let's revisit some fundamentals about Capability and Capacity. Each of us knows our strengths and has the urge to explore new areas to develop further. Let's call our current strengths existing capabilities and the new areas we want to explore possible capabilities.

Similarly, we all possess different levels of capacity. It could be the capacity to lift weights, run long distances, read extensively, or work tirelessly. It's beneficial to list down our existing capabilities and capacities, alongside what we aspire to achieve or develop as possible capabilities and capacities. Once we've identified these, prioritize and choose three existing capabilities to focus on. Additionally, aim to increase the capacity within these capabilities. When it comes to our mental capacity, remember that the human mind has infinite potential, often underutilized in achieving our goals. To systematically enhance our capability and capacity, it's important to understand a few key terms— attention, concentration, and focus—which we discussed in the chapter on Focus. Mastering these concepts can significantly improve our ability to go beyond our current limits.

> Before you try to increase your willpower, try to decrease the friction in your environment."
>
> **– James Clear**

1. Courage and Overcoming Fear

When we talk about going beyond our current capabilities and stepping into new territories, courage and the ability to overcome fear stand as the twin pillars of this journey. Courage is the force that pushes us forward, while overcoming fear is the process that allows us to break through barriers. Imagine standing at the edge of a cliff, looking down into an unknown abyss. The fear of the unknown grips you, but it's the courage within that urges you to take that leap of faith. This leap is not reckless; it is a calculated decision to move beyond the safety of the familiar and explore the potential that lies ahead.

Courage isn't the absence of fear; rather, it's the willingness to act despite fear. It means confronting our fears head-on, whether they are fears of failure, rejection, or the unknown. Each time we face and overcome a fear, we expand our comfort zone, making the previously daunting tasks more manageable. Think of the first time you tried something new—be it learning to ride a bike, speaking in public, or starting a new job. The initial fear was palpable, but as you persisted, that fear diminished, replaced by a sense of accomplishment and growth. This is the essence of going beyond: continuously challenging our limits and embracing new experiences.

For instance, consider public speaking. Many people rank it as their number one fear. However, those who muster the courage to speak publicly, despite their initial fear, often find that each experience builds confidence and reduces fear. Over time, what once seemed terrifying becomes a platform for growth and expression. Courage also plays a critical role in personal development. It encourages us to take risks and step out of our comfort zones, which is essential for achieving our long-term goals. Without courage, we tend to stick to what we know, missing out on opportunities for growth and self-discovery.

Overcoming fear involves acknowledging it, understanding its roots, and gradually exposing oneself to the feared situation in a controlled and progressive manner. This process, often referred to as exposure therapy in psychological terms, helps desensitize the fear response. It's about breaking down the fear into manageable steps and tackling them one at a time. For example, if someone fears starting a new business due to the risk involved, they can start by researching and learning about entrepreneurship. Next, they might attend networking events to meet other entrepreneurs. Gradually, they can take small steps toward launching their business, each step building their confidence and reducing their fear.

Going beyond requires a blend of courage to initiate action and strategies to overcome fear. Both are essential for personal and professional growth. Embracing courage and overcoming fear allows us to step into new experiences, challenge personal limits, and unlock our full potential.

Key Takeaways

Understanding courage and overcoming fear are essential for personal growth and expanding one's capabilities. Courage is not the absence of fear but the willingness to act despite it, pushing us to explore new experiences and step out of our comfort zones. Overcoming fear involves gradually confronting and desensitizing ourselves to the things that scare us, building confidence with each step. By embracing these principles, we can continually challenge our limits and achieve greater success and fulfillment in life. This approach transforms fear from a barrier into a stepping stone for growth.

2. Expanding Horizons through Risk-Taking and New Experiences

Expanding one's horizons is a fundamental aspect of personal and professional development. It involves deliberately stepping out of your comfort zone, embracing new experiences, and taking calculated risks that can lead to significant growth. This approach not only enriches your life narrative but also pushes the boundaries of what you know and can achieve. Consider the importance of seeking diverse experiences. When you immerse yourself in different cultures, perspectives, and activities, you gain a broader understanding of the world and its complexities. This broad exposure enhances your empathy, adaptability, and problem-solving skills. For instance, traveling to a new country and interacting with locals can provide insights into different ways of living and thinking. Learning a new language opens up new communication channels and cultural understanding. Trying out new hobbies or sports can reveal hidden talents and interests that you might never have discovered otherwise.

Taking calculated risks is another essential element in expanding your horizons. Risk-taking doesn't mean acting recklessly; rather, it involves making informed decisions that have the potential to lead to substantial growth and new opportunities. Entrepreneurs, for example, often take financial risks when starting new ventures. They face the uncertainty of the market, but through careful planning, resilience, and innovation, they can achieve remarkable success and contribute to societal advancement. Similarly, professionals who step outside their usual responsibilities to take on challenging projects demonstrate initiative and a willingness to grow, which can lead to career advancement and personal fulfillment. Pushing personal and professional boundaries through new experiences can also lead to discovering hidden talents and passions. Engaging in activities outside your routine can spark creativity and provide a sense of achievement. For example, someone who decides to take up painting might discover a latent artistic talent, leading to a fulfilling hobby or even a new career path. Similarly, participating in a public speaking course can help overcome the fear of speaking in front of an audience, boosting confidence and communication skills.

In professional settings, seeking new challenges and responsibilities is crucial for growth. Taking on projects outside your usual scope not only demonstrates your capability but also builds your skills and resilience. It shows your commitment to continuous learning and improvement, making you a valuable asset to any organization. This proactive approach can open doors to new career opportunities, promotions, and professional recognition. Moreover, expanding your horizons through new experiences fosters innovation. When you expose yourself to different fields and ideas, you can connect seemingly unrelated concepts to create novel solutions. This interdisciplinary approach is often the source of groundbreaking innovations and advancements. For instance, the field of biotechnology thrives on the intersection of biology and technology, leading to medical breakthroughs that save lives.

In essence, expanding your horizons through risk-taking and new experiences is about enriching your life and pushing beyond your current limitations. It involves embracing the unfamiliar, making thoughtful decisions to step into new territories, and continuously seeking growth. This mindset ensures that life remains dynamic, filled with opportunities for personal and professional development. It encourages you to view the world with curiosity and courage, transforming challenges into stepping stones for a more fulfilling and accomplished life. By adopting this approach, you not only enhance your own capabilities but also inspire those around you to embrace growth and change. This collective spirit of exploration and innovation can lead to a more vibrant, resilient, and progressive society. So, take that leap, try something new, and watch how your world expands in ways you never imagined.

Key Takeaways

Expanding your horizons through risk-taking and new experiences is essential for personal and professional growth. It involves stepping out of your comfort zone to engage with diverse activities and perspectives, which enhances empathy, adaptability, and problem-solving skills. Taking calculated risks can lead to significant opportunities and uncover hidden talents, pushing your personal and professional boundaries. Engaging in new challenges and responsibilities fosters innovation and interdisciplinary thinking, leading to creative solutions and advancements. By embracing this mindset, you enrich your life, inspire those around you, and contribute to a more dynamic and progressive society.

Embracing Change and Innovation

Embracing change and fostering innovation is essential for growth and adaptability. Change can be daunting, but it opens doors to new opportunities and experiences. For individuals, this means staying open to learning new skills and adapting to evolving circumstances. For organizations, fostering a culture of innovation can lead to groundbreaking advancements and maintain a competitive edge. Being proactive in seeking innovative solutions and viewing change as a positive force allows both individuals and organizations to stay dynamic and forward-thinking. Embracing change involves staying informed, being open-minded, encouraging experimentation, fostering collaboration, and quickly adapting to new circumstances.

Setting and Pursuing Audacious Goals

Setting high, ambitious goals is crucial for personal and professional growth. These goals act as a guiding star, directing efforts and inspiring progress. Overcoming limiting beliefs and aiming high pushes individuals to reach their full potential. Such aspirations require breaking down large goals into manageable steps and maintaining perseverance in the face of challenges. Audacious goals drive motivation and provide a clear sense of direction, leading to significant achievements and continuous personal development.

Key Tools and Techniques

Here are some widely appliedconcepts that can help you develop a persepctive

Blue Ocean Strategy

The Blue Ocean Strategy is a business approach that emphasizes creating new market spaces, termed "blue oceans," that are uncontested and free from competition, rather than competing in existing markets, known as "red oceans." This strategy encourages innovation and the identification of untapped opportunities, allowing organizations to make competition irrelevant. To implement the Blue Ocean Strategy, businesses begin by identifying unmet needs of potential customers or by redefining market boundaries. This involves looking beyond current demand and considering non-customers—individuals who could become customers if their needs were innovatively met. The strategy aims to break the trade-off between differentiation and low cost, enabling new avenues for growth.

A classic example of the Blue Ocean Strategy is Cirque du Soleil. By merging elements of theater and circus, they created a unique entertainment experience that appealed to a broader audience. They reduced costs by eliminating animal acts and focusing on a sophisticated theatrical experience, which attracted a more affluent demographic willing to pay higher ticket prices. Leveraging the Blue Ocean Strategy allows individuals and organizations to shift their focus from competing within existing markets to creating new opportunities where they can thrive without direct competition. This approach fosters innovation, customer satisfaction, and sustainable growth by exploring uncharted territories.

10x Thinking

10x Thinking is a mindset that encourages setting goals that are 10 times greater than what is typically considered achievable. This approach pushes individuals and organizations to think beyond incremental improvements and aim for exponential growth, driving extraordinary outcomes. Adopting 10x Thinking involves questioning the status quo and challenging existing limitations. Instead of asking, "How can we improve by 10%?" the focus shifts to, "How can we achieve 10 times more?" This radical rethinking often leads to groundbreaking innovations and significant advancements.

For example, Google's approach to projects and innovations embodies 10x Thinking. Rather than improving search engine speed by a small margin, they aim to make information universally accessible and useful, leading to the creation of products like Google Maps and self-driving cars. By setting ambitious goals, they push the boundaries of what is possible and open new frontiers in technology and service. Practicing 10x Thinking encourages creativity, risk-taking, and a visionary mindset. It propels individuals and organizations to strive for significant achievements and transformative impact, moving beyond incremental progress to monumental success.

Kaizen

Kaizen, a Japanese term meaning "continuous improvement," is a philosophy that focuses on making small, incremental changes consistently over time to achieve significant improvements. This approach is rooted in the belief that ongoing, minor enhancements can lead to substantial progress and efficiency. The Kaizen philosophy involves everyone in an organization, from top management to frontline workers, in identifying areas for improvement and implementing small changes. It encourages a culture of constant learning, experimentation, and refinement, promoting the idea that there is always room for improvement.

In practice, Kaizen might involve streamlining processes, reducing waste, enhancing productivity, or improving quality. For instance, Toyota's production system is renowned for its application of Kaizen principles, where workers continuously seek ways to optimize manufacturing processes and eliminate inefficiencies. Kaizen fosters a proactive mindset and a commitment to excellence. By embracing continuous incremental improvement, individuals and organizations can adapt to changing conditions, enhance their capabilities, and achieve sustained success. This approach underscores the value of persistence, attention to detail, and collective effort in driving long-term growth and innovation.

> "The man who does more than what he is paid for will soon be paid for more than what he does."
>
> **– Napoleon Hill**

Final Thoughts

Going beyond is more than just a concept; it's a fundamental drive that propels humanity forward. It's what has taken us from the age of stone tools to the digital era, pushing the boundaries of what we thought possible. This chapter aimed to ignite that spark within you, encouraging you to stretch beyond your comfort zone, embrace change, and take calculated risks. Adopting a mindset of continuous exploration transforms challenges into opportunities for innovation. When you view obstacles not as barriers but as stepping stones, you begin to see every situation as a chance to grow and surpass your current limitations. Remember, the greatest achievements come from those who dare to go beyond the ordinary and strive for the extraordinary.

By embracing this mindset, you're not just enhancing your personal growth; you're contributing to the progress of humanity as a whole. So, take the lessons learned here, apply them to your life, and let your journey of going beyond begin. Each step you take in pushing your boundaries sets a new precedent for what is possible, inspiring others to follow in your path.

> "The edge is in the inputs."
>
> The person who consumes from better sources gets better thoughts. The person who asks better questions gets better answers. The person who builds better habits gets better results.
>
> It's not the outcomes. It's the inputs."
>
> **– James Clear**

Going Beyond

1. Identifying Opportunities* and taking Initiatives**

Opportunity	Initiative

*Keep listing them down irrespective of whether you take initiative or not

**Where you took initiative, write down action plans

NOTES

What did I learn?

‘

‘

‘

‘

What will I do differently?

‘

‘

‘

‘

‘

Chapter 8
Learnings

"Every skill you have today was once unknown to you."

The human brain is a learning machine. Stick with it."

– James Clear

Introduction

"If you're not willing to learn, no one can help you. If you're determined to learn, no one can stop you."

– Zig Ziglar.

Learning is the mother of all skills, a lifelong journey that fuels personal and professional growth. It's not just about absorbing new information; it's about cultivating the ability to adapt, evolve, and excel in all facets of life. Learning shapes our experiences and our responses to them, guiding us toward better decision-making and enriched understanding. Learning is a lifelong process. Applying learnings is an every-minute process which continues lifelong. How we failed in our planning or what were the pitfalls will give us learnings to move forward. Every time we say yes instead of no, we learn. Every time you respond without listening to another person, you learn. When life presents an opportunity and you refuse to go beyond and grab it, you learn. It's not just a saying that one learns more from failures than anything else, it's a fact. When you fail to recognize potential inside you and later regret it in life, you learn. But when you make the process of learning a habit, you will have fewer regrets and you bounce back from your learnings.

Maintaining a learning log or failure log vis-à-vis your planned aspirations is an effective way to monitor yourself. This practice doesn't require any external help; it is a self-driven tool that fosters continuous improvement. By regularly documenting our experiences, both successes and setbacks, we create a tangible record of our growth. This log serves as a mirror, reflecting our progress and illuminating areas that need improvement. Periodically reviewing these logs allows us to learn from our actions and make informed decisions about our future. Finally, reviewing learnings from time to time and learning from your learnings will go a long way in benefiting you more than mastering any other skill in life. The means of learning are abundant. It's the desire to learn that is scarce. Naval Ravikant once said, 'The more you learn, the more you are exposed to the immense unknown." This should be empowering, not frightening. Embrace your ignorance and embrace lifelong learning.

Admitting you don't know something (yet) doesn't diminish your self-confidence; it only shows your humility and openness to learning new things. Adam Grant highlights that acknowledging our ignorance is a sign of intellectual humility. "Anyone who isn't embarrassed of who they were last year probably isn't learning enough," says Alain de Botton. This sentiment emphasizes the constant evolution of our knowledge and understanding. A mind that is full of conclusions is a dead mind; it is not a living mind. A living mind is a free mind, always learning and never concluding, as Jiddu Krishnamurti points out.

Alex Spanos once said, "The best way to learn is by doing. The only way to build a strong work ethic is by getting your hands dirty." This statement highlights the undeniable value of experiential learning. It's not just about absorbing information but actively engaging with tasks and challenges to gain a deeper, more practical understanding. When we dive into activities headfirst, every hands-on experience reinforces the knowledge we acquire, making it more tangible and lasting. Think about learning to ride a bicycle. You can read about balance, watch videos on pedaling techniques, and listen to advice from seasoned cyclists. However, nothing compares to the actual experience of getting on the bike and navigating through your first wobbly rides. The falls, the adjustments, and the eventual mastery are all integral parts of the learning process. Each time you practice, you are not only improving your skills but also solidifying your understanding of how to maintain balance, steer, and pedal simultaneously.

This approach applies to all areas of life, from professional skills to personal hobbies. In the workplace, taking on projects and responsibilities, even those outside your comfort zone, accelerates your learning curve. You might make mistakes along the way, but these mistakes are invaluable learning opportunities that theoretical knowledge alone cannot provide. By tackling real-world challenges, you develop problem-solving skills, adaptability, and resilience—qualities that are essential for success. In personal development, experiential learning can transform abstract concepts into concrete experiences. For instance, if you want to develop better public speaking skills, the best way to improve is to speak in front of an audience. You will learn more from one live presentation, with its unique challenges and immediate feedback, than from countless hours of reading about public speaking techniques. Moreover, this method of learning fosters a strong work ethic. When you engage actively with your tasks, you develop a sense of ownership and responsibility. You learn the value of persistence, the importance of attention to detail, and the satisfaction of seeing a project through to completion. These experiences build character and instill a strong work ethic that will serve you well in all aspects of life.

Learning by doing transforms theoretical knowledge into practical wisdom. It bridges the gap between knowing and understanding, making the learning process more effective and enriching. As we immerse ourselves in experiences and challenges, we not only gain skills and knowledge but also build the work ethic and resilience necessary to thrive in any endeavor. All that happens to us, including our humiliations, our misfortunes, and our embarrassments, are given to us as raw material, as clay, so that we may shape our art, according to Jorge Luis Borges. These experiences become the foundation upon which we build our skills and wisdom. Shane Parrish wisely noted, "The most practical skill in life is learning to do things when you don't feel like doing them. Anyone can do it when it's easy, but most people drop out the minute it gets hard." This highlights the importance of perseverance in the face of difficulty. The beautiful thing about learning is that nobody can take it away from you. The wisdom paradox illustrates that the more you learn, the more you realize how much you don't know. This should be a motivator, encouraging us to keep learning and growing.

"Anyone who stops learning is old, whether at twenty or eighty. Anyone who keeps learning stays young. The greatest thing in life is to keep your mind young," said Henry Ford. This underscores the vitality and rejuvenation that continuous learning brings into our lives. Your outcomes are a lagging measure of your habits. Your net worth is a lagging measure of your financial habits. Your weight is a lagging measure of your eating habits. Your knowledge is a lagging measure of your learning habits. Your clutter is a lagging measure of your cleaning habits. You get what you repeat. James Clear' insights remind us that our consistent actions determine our long-term success. Every skill you have was once unknown to you. The human brain is a learning machine. Stick with it. This simple yet profound statement encourages persistence in our learning journey. Your most unhappy customers are your greatest source of learning, as Bill Gates highlights. Embrace feedback, even when it's negative, as it offers the most valuable lessons for improvement. Learning shapes not only our knowledge but also our character. It helps us navigate through the complexities of life with greater ease and understanding. The process of learning involves an open mind, willing to accept new ideas and discard outdated ones. As we evolve, our learning evolves with us, adapting to new circumstances and environments. This dynamic process keeps us relevant and capable of handling the challenges that come our way.

One of the most powerful aspects of learning is its ability to transform failures into stepping stones for success. When we fail, it's an opportunity to learn what doesn't work and to refine our approach. This resilience builds a robust foundation for future endeavors, making each setback a valuable lesson rather than a defeat. Learning is the cornerstone of personal and professional growth. It's a lifelong journey that enriches our lives and equips us to face challenges with confidence and resilience. By cultivating a learning mindset, embracing failures as opportunities, and persistently seeking knowledge, we transform our lives and the world around us. Embrace every opportunity to learn, for it is through learning that we truly grow and achieve greatness.

Learnings

1. Learning Log

Errors / Mistakes	Learning and Action plan

2. Learning from others

Learning	How is this useful to me and what's my action

3. Monthly review of 1 and 2

What worked	What didn't

– How can I improve

NOTES

What did I learn?

-

-

-

-

-

What will I do differently?

-

-

-

-

-

Summary of concepts / models / frameworks that will be useful

Here is the list of essential concepts, models , theories and frameworks that form the foundation of basic management skills. While of some of them have been covered in earlier chapters, I am trying to summarize all of them here

1. SMART goals

2. Eisenhower Matrix

3. SWOT analysis

4. PDCA cycle

5. Maslow's Hierarchy of Needs

6. Five dysfunctions of a team

7. Pareto principle[80/20 rule]

8. GROW model [Goal, Reality, Options, Will]

9. Inversion Thinking [Charlie Munger]

10. Regret Minimization Framework [Jeff Bezos]

11. The 5 Whys Framework [Sakichi Toyoda]

12. First Principles Thinking [Elon Musk]

13. The Circle of Competence [Warren Buffet and Charlie Munger]

14. Second order thinking [Howard Marks]

15. 10/10/10 Rule[Suzy Welch]

16. Parkinson's Law

17. The law of diminishing returns

18. Occam's Razor

19. The four burners theory [James Clear]

20. Six Thinking Hats [Edward de Bono]

21.   Theory of Constraints[Eliyahu M Goldratt]

22.   The OODA loop [OBSERVE, Orient, Decide, Act]

23.   The Kano model [Noriaki Kano]

As you can see from the above list, there are many ways to approach a problem or institute a system

Being aware of these concepts helps us approach problem solving from different perspectives. Also, it will help us manage teams, scale up business activities and attain overall efficiencies

Chapter 9
Credibility

> "It takes 20 years to build a reputation and 5 minutes to ruin it. If you think about that, you'll do things differently."

– Warren Buffett.

Introduction

Credibility is the bedrock upon which trust is built and it's a vital aspect of both personal and professional realms. Imagine your credibility as a delicate sculpture, painstakingly crafted over time with care and precision. Every action, every word and every decision you make adds to this sculpture. Yet, a single misstep can shatter it in an instant, underscoring the importance of maintaining a strong, unwavering foundation. In our personal lives, credibility is what allows us to build meaningful and lasting relationships. When people trust us, they are more likely to confide in us, support us and stand by us during challenging times. Professionally, credibility can be the difference between a thriving career and a stagnant one. Colleagues, clients and superiors look for individuals they can rely on, whose words match their actions and who uphold a consistent standard of integrity and reliability.

As we delve into this chapter, we will explore the key elements that contribute to building and maintaining credibility. From honesty and integrity to reliability and accountability, we'll examine how these principles play out in real-life scenarios. We'll also discuss how to repair credibility if it has been damaged and how to ensure that your actions consistently reinforce the trust others place in you. Credibility isn't just about avoiding mistakes; it's about actively demonstrating your values and commitments through your behavior. As George Washington wisely noted, "It is better to offer no excuse than a bad one." This chapter aims to provide you with the tools and insights needed to build a solid reputation that stands the test of time, ensuring that you are seen as trustworthy and dependable in all aspects of your life.

1. Building Trust Through Consistency and Honesty

Building trust is like constructing a bridge that connects you to others. Each act of honesty and consistency adds a plank to that bridge, making it sturdier over time. Trust doesn't develop overnight; it is the result of repeated actions that demonstrate reliability and integrity. When you consistently show up, keep your promises and act with transparency, people begin to see you as dependable. This reliability is crucial in fostering both personal and professional relationships. Honesty is at the heart of trust. Being truthful, even when it's challenging, shows that you value integrity over convenience. It's not just about avoiding lies; it's about being genuine in all your interactions. For instance, if you make a mistake, admitting it openly instead of hiding it can actually strengthen trust. People appreciate honesty and the courage it takes to admit faults.

Integrity means aligning your actions with your values, doing the right thing even when no one is watching. This steadfast adherence to a moral code builds credibility. People know they can count on you to act fairly and honorably. This is especially important in professional settings, where your reputation can have a significant impact on your career progression. Consistency in your actions reinforces this trust. When people see that your behavior doesn't waver based on circumstances, they feel secure in their interactions with you. For example, consistently meeting deadlines and delivering quality work shows your colleagues and clients that you are reliable.

In every interaction, maintaining honesty and consistency helps to build a solid foundation of trust. This foundation not only strengthens relationships but also establishes you as a person of integrity, someone others can depend on. Imagine a scenario where you consistently deliver on your promises at work. Your colleagues and managers see you as reliable because your actions match your words. If you promise to complete a project by a specific deadline, you follow through. This builds a sense of trust and respect. Over time, your consistent performance makes you a go-to person for important tasks, as people know they can count on you.

On the other hand, if you are inconsistent, it can erode trust. If you occasionally fail to meet deadlines or don't follow through on commitments, people may start to question your reliability. Even a few instances of inconsistency can overshadow numerous instances of reliability. It's crucial to understand that trust is fragile; it takes a long time to build but can be easily damaged. Honesty also plays a critical role. When you're honest, even about uncomfortable truths, it shows that you value integrity. For instance, if you make a mistake on a project, admitting it and working to fix it rather than covering it up demonstrates accountability. This kind of honesty can actually enhance trust, as people appreciate your transparency and willingness to take responsibility.

In personal relationships, these principles are just as important. Being consistently honest and reliable strengthens bonds with family and friends. They know they can count on you, which builds a deep sense of trust and security. Whether it's being there when you promise to help a friend move or keeping confidences, these actions show that you are dependable and trustworthy. Overall, building trust through consistency and honesty requires a commitment to integrity and reliability in all areas of life. It's about showing up, being genuine and doing what you say you will do, day in and day out. This approach not only strengthens your relationships but also enhances your reputation as a person of integrity.

Key Takeaways

Building trust requires consistent and honest actions over time. Integrity is the backbone of trust; aligning your actions with your values strengthens your credibility. People appreciate honesty, even when it means admitting mistakes, as it demonstrates accountability and transparency. Consistency in behavior, whether in meeting deadlines or keeping promises, assures others of your reliability. Trust, once established, can significantly enhance both personal and professional relationships, but it is fragile and must be carefully maintained. Ultimately, trust is built through a commitment to integrity, reliability and genuine interactions.

2. Upholding Ethical Standards and Values

Upholding ethical standards and values acts as a guiding compass for our actions and decisions. These standards provide a framework that ensures our behavior aligns with both our personal principles and the expectations of the broader community. When we adhere to ethical values, we create a foundation of trust and respect with those around us, enhancing our credibility. For instance, maintaining honesty in all dealings, even when it is challenging, demonstrates a commitment to integrity that others can rely on. This kind of behavior signals to others that we can be trusted, as our actions consistently reflect our words. Ethical behavior in the workplace fosters a positive culture and encourages others to act with the same integrity. It's not just about following rules; it's about embodying principles like fairness, respect and responsibility in every action.

Ethics also play a crucial role in decision-making. When faced with difficult choices, an ethical framework helps navigate the complexities by prioritizing what is right over what is easy or expedient. This commitment to doing what is right, even when no one is watching, solidifies one's reputation and earns the trust of peers and the community. It ensures that decisions are made not just for short-term gains but with a long-term perspective that considers the well-being of others. In personal relationships, upholding values like honesty, loyalty, and empathy strengthens bonds and builds a solid foundation for mutual respect. By consistently acting in line with our values, we ensure that our behavior is predictable and trustworthy, which is essential for long-term relationships. People feel secure and valued when they know that our actions will consistently reflect our stated principles, which in turn fosters deeper connections and mutual respect.

Ethical standards and values are also critical in leadership. Leaders who prioritize ethics and values set a tone for their organizations, creating an environment where ethical behavior is the norm and not the exception. This can lead to a more motivated and engaged workforce, as employees see their leaders as role models who practice what they preach. It helps in building a culture of trust, where everyone feels accountable to uphold the same high standards. Ultimately, ethical standards and values are indispensable for maintaining credibility. They guide our actions, ensure alignment with our principles and help build a reliable, trustworthy reputation both personally and professionally. They are the bedrock upon which trust is built, allowing us to navigate our lives with integrity and earn the respect and trust of those around us.

Furthermore, adhering to ethical standards and values can enhance our personal growth and self-respect. When we consistently act according to our principles, we feel a sense of pride and satisfaction that reinforces our commitment to those values. This positive feedback loop strengthens our ethical resolve and helps us stay true to our moral compass, even when faced with temptation or pressure. In professional settings, upholding ethical standards can lead to long-term success and stability. Companies known for their ethical practices often enjoy greater customer loyalty, improved employee morale, and a stronger reputation in the marketplace. This ethical foundation can also protect against legal issues and scandals that can arise from unethical behavior, further securing the organization's future. Ethical standards and values are essential for building and maintaining credibility. They shape our actions, guide our decisions, and foster trust and respect in our relationships. By committing to these principles, we can navigate our personal and professional lives with integrity, earn the trust of those around us, and achieve lasting success and fulfillment.

Key Takeaways

Maintaining ethical standards and values is essential for building trust and credibility. These standards act as a guiding compass for our actions, ensuring they align with both personal principles and community expectations. Adhering to values like honesty, fairness, and responsibility fosters respect and trust in personal and professional relationships. Ethical behavior in decision-making prioritizes long-term well-being over short-term gains, reinforcing our reputation as reliable and trustworthy individuals. In leadership, setting a tone of integrity encourages a positive organizational culture, motivating others to follow suit. Ultimately, upholding ethics and values enhances personal growth, self-respect, and long-term success.

3. Impact of Credibility on Relationships and Opportunities

Credibility plays a pivotal role in shaping relationships, career opportunities and public perception. When people trust you, they are more likely to build strong, lasting relationships with you, whether in personal or professional settings. In the workplace, credibility can lead to career advancements, as trustworthiness and reliability are highly valued traits. Additionally, a credible reputation enhances public perception, opening doors to new opportunities and networks. Trustworthiness acts as a social currency that can significantly influence one's success and fulfillment.

4. Rebuilding Credibility After a Setback

Restoring credibility after it has been compromised is a challenging but essential task. Transparency and accountability are key strategies in this process. Being open about the mistake and taking responsibility for it shows integrity and a commitment to making amends. Actions should align with words to rebuild trust gradually. Demonstrating consistent, positive behavior over time helps to restore confidence and credibility in the eyes of others. A sincere effort to learn from setbacks and prevent future occurrences also reinforces the regained trust.

5. Ethics, Transparency and Reputation Management

Ethical practices and transparency are fundamental to maintaining and managing a positive reputation. Adhering to ethical standards ensures actions are aligned with moral principles, which build respect and trust. Transparency in operations and decisions fosters an environment of openness and honesty, further strengthening credibility. Effective reputation management involves consistently upholding these values, addressing issues promptly and communicating openly with stakeholders. This approach not only preserves credibility but also enhances it, promoting long-term success and integrity in all endeavors.

House of Cards

Imagine building a house of cards. Each card must be placed with utmost care and precision, balancing delicately to form a stable structure. One wrong move, one misplaced card, and the entire house collapses. This is a perfect metaphor for credibility. When we start building our credibility, each action, decision, and word acts like a card in this intricate structure. Consistent, honest behavior forms a solid foundation, while ethical standards and transparency add stability to our growing reputation. Just as a house of cards requires a steady hand and careful placement, maintaining credibility demands ongoing effort and mindfulness.

Consider a time when someone lost your trust. Perhaps it was a colleague who promised to meet a deadline but repeatedly failed, or a friend who wasn't honest about something significant. Each of these incidents is like a gust of wind, threatening the stability of the house of cards. Rebuilding that trust isn't easy; it requires deliberate, consistent actions to place each card back carefully. In professional settings, credibility can be the difference between success and failure. For instance, a manager who consistently meets deadlines, communicates transparently and stands by their team builds a reputation as a reliable and trustworthy leader. This credibility opens up opportunities for promotions and new projects. Conversely, a leader who frequently misses deadlines, hides mistakes, or shifts blame can quickly lose the trust of their team and superiors, much like a house of cards falling apart.

In personal relationships, credibility nurtures deep, meaningful connections. Imagine promising a friend that you'll help them move, but then backing out last minute without a good reason. This action is akin to pulling a critical card from your house, causing it to wobble. Over time, if such actions continue, the entire structure of trust and respect can crumble. However, credibility isn't just about maintaining a perfect record. It's also about how we handle setbacks. When the house of cards collapses, we can either give up or start rebuilding with renewed focus and determination. Taking responsibility for mistakes, being transparent about them and making sincere efforts to rectify the situation can slowly but surely rebuild trust. This is where the true strength of credibility lies—in the ability to bounce back and rebuild stronger.

Building and maintaining credibility is a continuous, deliberate process. Each action, like each card, matters. By prioritizing honesty, consistency and ethical behavior, we can construct a robust and resilient house of credibility, capable of withstanding the inevitable challenges that come our way.

Key Tools and Techniques

Ethical Leadership

Ethical leadership involves guiding an organization or community based on core ethical principles, fostering an environment of trust and credibility. Leaders who prioritize ethics ensure their actions are aligned with their stated values, setting a standard for others to follow. This alignment helps build a culture where ethical behavior is the norm and trust is a natural outcome.

To practice ethical leadership, one must:

1. **Lead by Example**: Demonstrate integrity and ethical behaviour in all actions, showing commitment to values even when it is challenging.

2. **Communicate Openly**: Maintain transparency with team members and stakeholders. Honest communication fosters trust and prevents misunderstandings.

3. **Make Fair Decisions**: Ensure decisions are made based on fairness and justice, considering the impact on all stakeholders.

4. **Hold Accountability**: Establish a system where ethical breaches are addressed promptly and appropriately, ensuring everyone is held to the same standards.

5. **Encourage Ethical Behaviour**: Promote an rganizational culture that rewards ethical behaviour and supports employees in making ethical decisions.

By embedding ethical practices into leadership, trust is built over time, enhancing the leader's credibility and the organization's reputation.

Social Proof

Social proof is a psychological phenomenon where people look to the actions and behaviors of others to guide their own decisions. In the context of credibility, social proof can significantly impact how an individual or organization is perceived. When people see others trusting and endorsing a person or brand, they are more likely to trust and follow suit.

There are several ways to leverage social proof:

1. **Testimonials and Reviews**: Positive feedback from customers or clients can serve as powerful endorsements, building trust among potential clients.

2. **Case Studies**: Sharing detailed stories of how your products or services have helped others can provide compelling evidence of your credibility.

3. **Endorsements**: Support from respected figures or organisations can enhance your reputation and attract more trust from the public.

4. **User Numbers**: Displaying large numbers of users or subscribers can indicate popularity and reliability, encouraging others to join.

5. **Media Coverage**: Being featured in reputable media outlets can provide third-party validation and enhance credibility.

By effectively using social proof, you can build a solid foundation of trust and enhance your reputation, encouraging others to engage with and support you.

Honesty Box

The honesty box concept is a method used to gauge and build trust within a community or customer base by allowing individuals to pay based on trust. This technique involves placing products or services where people can take them and leave payment voluntarily, without direct supervision. It relies on the honor system and fosters an environment of mutual trust and respect.

To implement an honesty box system:

1. **Set Clear Expectations**: Clearly communicate the expectations and trust placed in the users or customers. Signage explaining the system can help.

2. **Start Small**: Begin with low-cost items to minimise risk and build trust gradually.

3. **Monitor and Adjust**: Track the honesty levels and adjust the system as needed. If dishonesty is detected, consider implementing measures to improve accountability.

4. **Encourage Participation:** Highlight the community aspect and the importance of mutual trust. Positive reinforcement can encourage honest behavior.

5. **Share Success Stories**: Publicize instances where the honesty box has worked well, reinforcing the trust and credibility within the community.

Using an honesty box can be a powerful way to build trust, demonstrating faith in people's integrity and fostering a culture of honesty and credibility.

These tools and techniques provide a robust framework for building and maintaining credibility, emphasizing the importance of ethical leadership, leveraging social proof, and fostering trust through transparency and honesty.

Final Thoughts

Credibility is a crucial yet delicate asset that influences every facet of life. It is the bedrock upon which trust is built, whether in personal relationships, professional environments, or within the broader community. As Warren Buffett wisely noted, it takes years to build a reputation but only moments to ruin it. This underscores the continual effort required to maintain credibility through consistent, ethical and transparent behavior.

> "The strength of a nation derives from the integrity of the home."
>
> **– Confucius**

This profound insight highlights that the values and integrity practiced within our homes form the foundation for the broader societal trust and credibility. By fostering ethical behavior, honesty and transparency within our families and immediate circles, we contribute to a stronger, more trustworthy society.

Ultimately, maintaining credibility requires a proactive approach to reputation management. It involves being mindful of our actions, consistently aligning them with our values and taking responsibility when we fall short. By doing so, we not only enhance our own trustworthiness but also contribute positively to the communities we are a part of, reinforcing the integral connection between personal integrity and societal strength.

Credibility

Questions to ask on a regular basis

• Am I meeting Timelines consistently [Performer]

• Am I Communicating delays etc., [Transparent]

• Did I Come out with alternate plans [Providing solutions]

• Can I consider myself as Knowledgeable person ; did I add anything to my skills [Knowledge; Skill]

• Did I take new Initiatives [Going Beyond]

• Am I Open to ideas [Open]

• Do I listen and do I have clarity in my communication [Communication]

NOTES

What did I learn?

`

`

`

`

`

What will I do differently?

`

`

`

`

`

Conclusion

As I sit down to conclude this book, I am reminded of the journey we have taken together—a journey through the essential skills that shape our lives and define our successes. Each chapter represents a stepping stone toward a more fulfilling and effective life, a life where planning and learning are the pillars upon which we build our dreams and ambitions.

Planning is the father of all skills because it lays the groundwork for everything we aspire to achieve. It is the roadmap that guides us, the strategy that aligns our actions with our goals. From setting clear objectives to prioritizing our tasks, planning ensures that we move forward with purpose and direction. It is through meticulous planning that we pave the way for success, making the seemingly impossible attainable. Without a solid plan, even the best of intentions can falter, much like a house built without a sturdy foundation.

Learning, on the other hand, is the mother of all skills. It nurtures our minds and souls, fostering growth and resilience. Embracing a mindset of continuous improvement and lifelong learning allows us to adapt, innovate, and overcome challenges. Every failure becomes a lesson, every obstacle an opportunity to grow. The thirst for knowledge and the willingness to learn are what propel us beyond our current limitations, opening doors to new possibilities and achievements. Learning nourishes and sustains our intellectual and emotional growth like a mother, enabling us to evolve and thrive in an ever-changing world.

Together, planning and learning give birth to credibility, the child of our efforts and endeavors. Credibility is the trust we earn through consistent, honest actions. It is the reputation we build over time, the foundation upon which relationships and opportunities are built. Without credibility, our plans and learning hold little value in the eyes of others. It is the cornerstone of personal and professional success, a testament to our integrity and reliability.

Throughout this book, we have explored various skills that contribute to building credibility. Time management, prioritizing tasks, and managing our time effectively enhance our reliability. Clear and empathetic communication fosters trust and understanding. Positive behaviors and habits reinforce our character and dependability. Concentrated efforts on our goals demonstrate our commitment and drive. Embracing challenges and learning from failures show resilience and adaptability. Pushing our boundaries and taking risks highlight our courage and ambition.

If we plan well and learn well, credibility is the natural outcome. It is the visible manifestation of our efforts, the measure of our success. Credibility is the foundation that can make or break us. It determines how others perceive us and how we navigate the complex web of personal and professional relationships.

In Chapter 1, we delved into planning, the father of all skills. We saw how setting goals, prioritizing tasks, and managing time can provide a clear path forward. We learned that a well-thought-out plan not only guides us but also gives us the confidence to tackle our goals head-on.

Chapter 2, introduced us to various concepts of time management and how important it is to focus on quadrant 2 to realize our aspirations

In Chapter 3, we explored the critical skill of communication. We examined how active listening, empathetic communication, and nonverbal cues can enhance our interactions and build stronger relationships. Effective communication is essential for conveying our ideas, resolving conflicts, and fostering mutual understanding.

Chapter 4 focused on behavior and how our actions reflect our values and character. We discussed the importance of positive habits, emotional intelligence, and maintaining integrity. Our behavior shapes how others perceive us and impacts our credibility and trustworthiness.

In Chapter 5, we turned our attention to focus, the ability to concentrate on our goals and tasks. We explored techniques for improving concentration, managing distractions, and entering a state of deep work. Focus is crucial for achieving our aspirations and maintaining productivity.

Chapter 6 delved into the concept of a growth mindset. We discussed the importance of embracing challenges, learning from failures, and cultivating resilience. A growth mindset enables us to overcome obstacles and continually improve ourselves.

In Chapter 7, we explored the idea of going beyond, pushing our boundaries, and seeking new experiences. We discussed the importance of risk-taking, innovation, and setting ambitious goals. Going beyond our comfort zones allows us to achieve extraordinary feats and discover our true

Chapter 8 introduced us to the power of learning, the mother of all skills. We discussed the importance of adopting a growth mindset, embracing lifelong learning, and continually seeking new knowledge and experiences. Learning is the bedrock of personal growth and development, enabling us to adapt to changing circumstances and seize new opportunities.

Finally, in Chapter 9, we examined the importance of credibility. We discussed how consistent, ethical actions build trust and how maintaining credibility is essential for personal and professional success. Credibility is the foundation upon which our reputation is built, and it influences every aspect of our lives.

As we move forward, let us remember that building credibility is an ongoing process. It requires consistent effort, ethical behavior, and a commitment to continuous growth. Let us strive to be individuals who not only plan and learn but also inspire trust and respect in others. Thank you for embarking on this journey with me. May the skills and insights shared in this book guide you toward a life of purpose, growth, and unwavering credibility.

As we conclude, I encourage you to embrace these principles wholeheartedly. Let planning be the guiding force that directs your efforts. Let learning be the nurturing influence that fuels your growth. And let credibility be the cornerstone of your legacy. Strive to build a life of integrity and trustworthiness, where your actions speak louder than words and where your reputation is a testament to your character. Thank you for joining me on this journey. May the insights and strategies shared in this book empower you to create a life of purpose, growth, and unwavering credibility. Remember, the foundation you build today will shape your future and the legacy you leave behind.

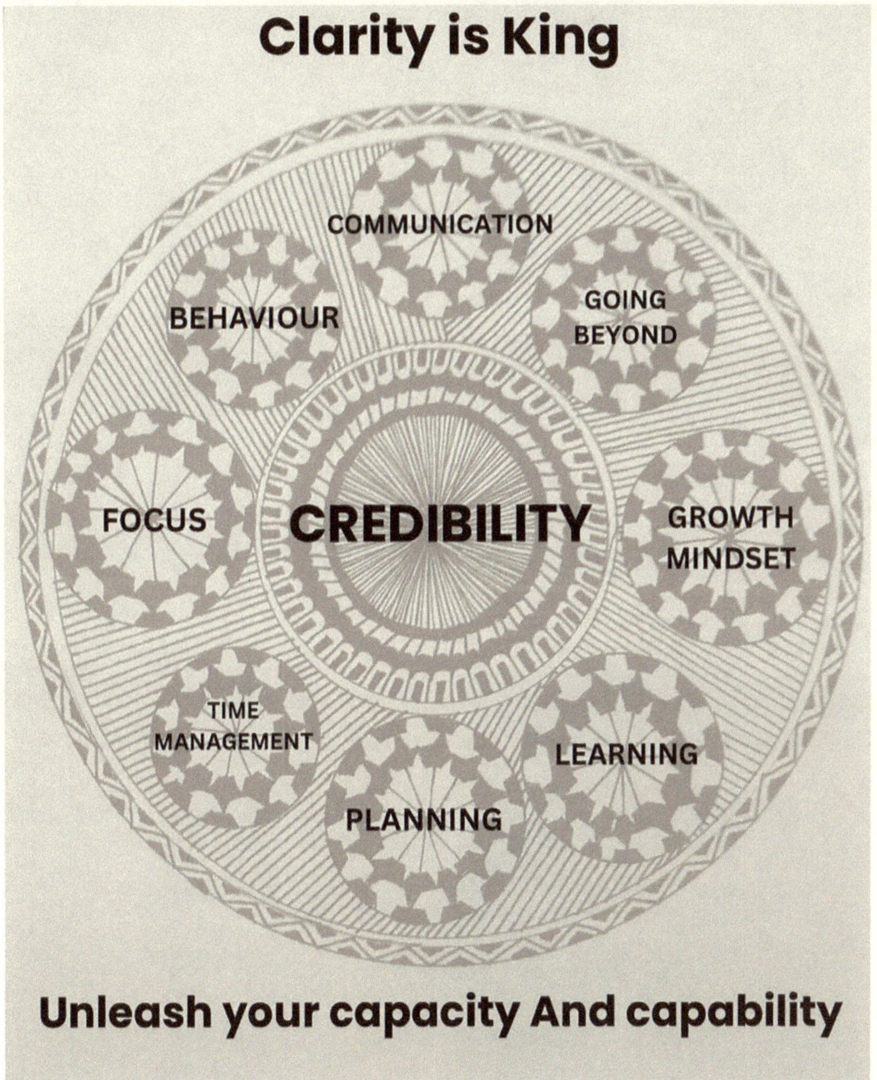

Clarity is King
COMMUNICATION
BEHAVIOUR
GOING BEYOND
FOCUS
CREDIBILITY
GROWTH MINDSET
TIME MANAGEMENT
PLANNING
LEARNING
Unleash your capacity And capability

References

a. Websites / blogs:

https://jamesclear.com/3-2-1

https://simonsinek.com/

https://www.robinsharma.com/

https://nav.al/

https://www.sahilbloom.com

https://billyoppenheimer.com/?amp

https://thedankoe.com/

https://ankurwarikoo.com/

https://fs.blog/

https://www.paulgraham.com/

https://kk.org/

https://adamgrant.net/

https://collabfund.com/blog/

https://www.morganhousel.com/

https://rajivtalreja.com/

b. Books:

1. Seven Habits of Highly Effective People – Stephen Covey

2. The Fifth Discipline – Peter Senge

3. Elon Musk – Ashlee Vance

4. The Talent Code – Daniel Coyle

5. Grit – Angela Duckworth

6. Hidden Potential - Adam Grant

7. Same As Ever - Morgan Housel

8. Atomic Habits - James Clear

9. Elon Musk - Walter Isaacson

10. The Daily Stoic - Ryan Holiday

11. The Almanac of Naval Ravikanth

12. Zero to One – Peter Thiel

13. The Everyday Hero – Robin Sharma